T0326372

The Sayings of Layman P'ang

The Sayings of
Layman P'ang

A Zen Classic of China

Translated by James Green

Foreword by Dennis Genpo Merzel Roshi
Preface by Keido Fukushima Roshi
Introduction by Jeff Shore
Illustrations by Michael Hofmann

SHAMBHALA
Boulder
2009

Shambhala Publications, Inc.
2129 13th Street
Boulder, Colorado 80302
www.shambhala.com

Shambhala Publications makes every effort to print on acid-free,
recycled paper.

Shambhala Publications is distributed worldwide by Penguin
Random House, Inc., and its subsidiaries.

Designed by James D. Skatges

Library of Congress Cataloging-in-Publication Data
Pang, Yun, ca. 740–808.
[Pang ju shi yu lu. English]
The sayings of layman P'ang: a Zen classic of China /
translated by James Green; foreword by Dennis Genpo Merzel;
preface by Keido Fukushima; illustrations by Michael Hofmann.
p. cm.
ISBN 978-1-59030-630-7 (pbk.: alk. paper)
1. Zen Buddhism—Early works to 1800.
I. Green, James Reid, 1948– II. Title.
BQ9265.P3613 2009
294.3'927—DC22
2008030702

Dedicated, with loving gratitude,
to Keido Fukushima Roshi

Contents

Foreword by Dennis Genpo Merzel Roshi   *xiii*
Preface by Keido Fukushima Roshi   *xvii*
Introduction by Jeff Shore   *xix*
Translator's Note   *xxxv*
Acknowledgments   *xxxix*

The Recorded Sayings of Layman P'ang   1

PROLOGUE   3

DIALOGUES WITH SHIH-T'OU (SEKITO)

1. Suddenly Stopping the World   13
2. Subtleties of Daily Life   15

DIALOGUES WITH MA-TSU (BASO)

3. One Gulp   17
4. A Distinctly Authentic Person   20
5. The Bone and Muscle of Water   21

DIALOGUES WITH YUEH-SHAN (YAKUSAN)

6. One Vehicle   23
7. Viewing the Snow   25

DIALOGUES WITH CH'I-FENG (ZAICHO)

8. There You Are   27
9. Front and Rear   29
10. The Distance to the Mountaintop   31
11. That Which Is Not Spoken   33

DIALOGUES WITH TAN-HSIA (TANKA)

12. Meeting Ling-chao   35
13. Deaf and Dumb   38
14. The Layman and Mr. P'ang   40
15. The Eye of the Heritage   41
16. The Head Scarf   42
17. Seven and One   44
18. Making Waves   45

DIALOGUES WITH PAI-LING (HYAKUREI)

19. Potent Instruction   49
20. Speaking and Not Speaking   51
21. What Did You Say?   52
22. The Eyes   53

DIALOGUES WITH P'U-CHI (FUZAI)

23. Haggling Over a Basket   55

24. Speaking Words   57

25. A Word from the Womb   59

26. Open or Closed?   61

DIALOGUE WITH CH'ANG-TZU (CHOSHI)

27. Not Violating the True Self   63

DIALOGUES WITH SUNG-SHAN (SHOZAN)

28. Why Don't You Say Something?   67

29. The Ox Doesn't Know   69

30. Sung-shan's Staff   70

31. Yellow Leaves and Green Leaves   72

32. Sung-shan's Ruler   74

DIALOGUES WITH PEN-HSI (HONGOKU)

33. Don't Tell Someone What to Do   77

34. Is This So, or Not?   79

DIALOGUE WITH TA-MEI (DAIBAI)

35. The Plum's Core   83

DIALOGUES WITH TA-YU (DAI'IKU)

36. Dining Etiquette   85

37. Fundamental Truth   87

DIALOGUES WITH TSE-CH'UAN (SOKUSEN)

38. Old and Young   89

39. The Intangible Dharma Body   91
40. Host and Guest   93

DIALOGUE WITH LO-P'U (RAKUHO)

41. Hot and Cold   95

DIALOGUES WITH SHIH-LIN (SEKIRIN)

42. Tan-hsia's Activities   97
43. Say It Succinctly   99
44. It's Indescribable   100

DIALOGUE WITH YANG-SHAN (KYOZAN)

45. Respected Mountain   101

DIALOGUE WITH KU-YIN (KOKUIN)

46. Wild Fox Zen   103

DIALOGUE WITH A MONK
WHILE READING THE SUTRAS

47. Reading the Sutras   105

DIALOGUE WITH A MONK
DOING RITUAL BEGGING

48. Accepting Charity   107

DIALOGUE WITH AN OXHERD

49. Where the Path Leads   109

DIALOGUE WITH A MEDITATION TEACHER
50. The Message of the *Diamond Sutra* 111

THREE VIEWS OF HARD AND EASY
51. Three Views of Hard and Easy 113

THREE-STANZA POEM
52. Three-Stanza Poem 115

DIALOGUES WITH LING-CHAO (REISHO)
53. Each Blade of Grass Is Clear-Cut 119
54. Helping Someone Up 120

THE LAYMAN'S DEATH
55. The Layman's Death 121

DIALOGUES FROM OTHER SOURCES
56. Tan-hsia's Rosary 123
57. Pen-hsi and the Skull 125
58. Mrs. P'ang Goes Back 127

Appendix: Brief Ancestor Chart 129

Foreword

Dennis Genpo Merzel Roshi

Layman P'ang continues to be an inspiration and a model within the Zen tradition twelve hundred years after his death, not only because of this colorful book you hold in your hands, but also because of what he represents. As a layperson who is regarded as both a living exemplar and a teacher of Zen, he is one of a line of outstanding human beings, men and women, renowned and obscure, stretching from the great contemporary of Shakyamuni Buddha, Vimalakirti, through Hui-neng, the pivotal Sixth Patriarch of Zen in China, to those who are reinvigorating Buddhism throughout the East and West in our own time. The very name by which we know him, "Layman P'ang," raises questions that are at least as old as Buddhism itself: What does it mean to be a layperson in Zen? What is the difference between a person who is ordained and one who is not?

In Buddhism the ceremony of ordination (in Japanese, *shukke tokudo*) marks the passage from layperson to what we call a monk, nun, or priest, though actually those Western terms do not have the same meanings in the East. *Tokudo* means "ceremony," and *shukke* is "leaving home." But *shukke* does not just signify leaving one's physical home; it is also the leaving of that comfortable place called the self, and the serving of something greater than ourselves. So one essential difference between being ordained and remaining a layperson is that the primary commitment of the ordained is really to serve others, which entails giving up their own personal comforts. As laypersons we can still commit ourselves to serving others. We can serve our community and the world at large without giving up our physical home or family or vocation. Actually, I think this is a more difficult practice than going off to a monastery and truly living as a monk.

In the West not too many of us so-called monks or priests actually live in monasteries. Most of us trained in Zen centers as residents and had children, families, and, in some cases, a job outside the centers. Most Zen teachers in the West—I wouldn't say all of us—trained and practiced, even as we were ordained, while raising families. That's why way back a long time ago Shunryu Suzuki Roshi, one of the early Japanese pioneers who brought Zen to America, said neither are we priests nor are we laypeople exactly. That's how I myself have felt for the thirty-five years since I received *shukke tokudo*. I'm not quite a priest, nor am I really a layperson. We are some perhaps indefinable thing that bridges these two worlds. Sometimes I've felt more aligned with the lay aspect and sometimes more with the monastic.

For the last fifteen years or so, I've realized the importance of having not only an ordained lineage but also a lay lineage and laypeople and lay practice—and that if we're going to make any difference in the world, it's going to be as laypeople. And personally, even though I've been ordained for many years now, I feel more like a layperson. I live a lay life. I've had children, I have a mortgage, I have a job, many jobs, and I think that people like Layman P'ang and Vimalakirti are wonderful examples of living as householders and having a practice too.

Layman P'ang himself seems to have spent some time in monasteries studying under great teachers. In the conversations with his ordained friends recorded in this book, even when the subject of ordainment is discussed, he treats the matter lightly and never gives explicit reasons for his choice to remain a layman. From the little we know about his life, it seems fair to say that he found, as we do today, that there are many obstacles in the world that make it difficult to pursue a path, but just because it's difficult doesn't make it impossible, and actually all the difficulties just become grist for the mill. Living a normal lay life while being a practitioner is a beautiful way to practice.

Layman P'ang's example accords with my experience. In my own life the distinction between monk and layperson is really not that relevant. Ever since I first entered the path in 1971, it's always been about clarifying the Way for myself in order to be able to offer clearer teachings and instructions to others, in order to be able to empower others. For the sake of others you feel a responsibility to be as clear as humanly possible. Even though I have given the Buddhist precepts to several hundred people and *shukke tokudo* to over a hundred, my primary goal is not to create Buddhists. Rather, I believe that we honor and sustain the legacy of our great forebears, lay and ordained alike, by spreading the essence of the buddhadharma to the world, even outside Buddhism. Layman P'ang's example, reflected in this classic book, inspires all of us in helping people to wake up and raise their level of consciousness, and in becoming better and more decent human beings who live and act with wisdom and compassion, rather than out of ignorance and greed and hatred.

March 2008
Kanzeon Zen Center
Salt Lake City, Utah

Preface

Keido Fukushima Roshi

It is a pleasure to present Jim Green's translation, *The Sayings of Layman P'ang*. Jim has been a lay disciple of mine since 1974. Able to read classical Chinese, he has previously translated *The Recorded Sayings of Zen Master Joshu*, and now the present translation has been completed.

P'ang is a Chinese layman akin to the renowned Indian Buddhist layman Vimalakirti. Layman P'ang's record, full of encounters with Zen monks, is a delightful and thrilling account. It is most appropriate that an American layman, Jim Green, has chosen to translate such a work.

While American Zen has certainly learned a great deal from Japanese Zen, I think it is now time for American Zen to stand on its own two feet. In contrast with the "monastic Zen" of Japan, American Zen is essentially a "lay Zen." I am delighted that *The Sayings of Layman P'ang* is now available for laymen and laywomen around the world, and hope that it will be read with care by many. I trust it will play a role in establishing and developing an authentic lay Zen in America.

October 2007
Keido Fukushima
Head Abbot of Tofukuji
Zen Master of Tofukuji Monastery

Introduction

Jeff Shore

Layman P'ang has been venerated in Asia for well over a thousand years. The publication of this book follows shortly upon the twelve-hundredth anniversary of his death in 808. Recently, the rest of the world has begun embracing him. The title song of Van Morrison's 1990 album, *Enlightenment,* opens with a refrain about chopping wood and carrying water. Borrowed from one of Layman P'ang's most famous poems, it expresses the Layman's newfound spiritual insight in terms of his daily actions (see Dialogue 2, where it is rendered a bit more accurately as "Collecting firewood and carrying water").

How could someone with no social standing or monastic rank inspire his countrymen for over a thousand years, and why does he stir people on the other side of the globe today? The following remarks provide background to better understand and appreciate *The Sayings of Layman P'ang*—

and maybe even to allow us to catch a glimpse of the man himself.

Classic Zen histories state:

> The great solitary one reigns *West-of-the-River,*
> The one on top of the rock rules *South-of-the-Lake.*
> Many travel from one to the other.
> Anyone who has not encountered these two
>   great men
> Is considered an ignoramus.

This was the scene at the time of Layman P'ang. "The great solitary one" refers to the great Ch'an master Ma-tsu; "[The one] on top of the rock" is the literal translation of Ch'an Master Shih-t'ou, whose name is taken from the flat rock on which he built his hut. These were the two great masters whom P'ang encountered.

Ma-tsu and Shih-t'ou were not just two exceptional monks living during an exceptional time in Chinese history: from them descends the teaching that flowered into what we now call the Rinzai and Soto schools of Zen Buddhism. And as we will see, the Layman truly encountered (not simply met) both of them.

The Layman naturally followed in these masters' footsteps by going beyond them: "Realization equaling the master's diminishes its worth by half; only realization surpassing the master's is worthy of continuing the lineage." This statement of Master Po-chang (Jpn.: Hyakujo), a leading dharma heir of Ma-tsu, is celebrated in the Zen tradition for expressing what is required of a worthy disciple.

The realization at issue—and what is vividly disclosed at the heart of these anecdotes—is the realization of Buddhism's basic truth of no-self (Pali: *anattan;* Skt: *anatman*). In the Indian Buddhist tradition, this truth was disclosed through meticulous meditations on and analyses of what constitutes "the world," within and without. The Zen tradition is known for directly pointing out no-self and developing the koan to foster abrupt awakening. Layman P'ang manifests this living truth in your face, stripped of Buddhist or Zen jargon, unmistakably clear and unadorned, for all to see. A pity that he did not become a monk and have plenty of worthy disciples to continue his lineage? Perhaps we are all his worthy disciples. The fundamental Way of the Buddha has always flowed freely and has been available to all people. Nothing, institutional or otherwise, can really obstruct it.

Despite his father's best attempts to shield him from the realities of life twenty-five hundred years ago, the layman called Gotama in Pali (Skt: Gautama) left all behind and followed the emerging tradition of wandering ascetics known as *samana* (Skt: *sramana*). After Gotama's awakening, the five ascetics who had formerly practiced austerities with him now followed his Path and, under his tutelage, realized it for themselves. Only then did they take a very simple ordination. According to the Pali canon, there were then in the world six *arahant* (Skt: *arhat*). The seventh *arahant* in the world was Yasa, the son of a wealthy family. His father, mother, and wife all entered the Path as lay disciples.

Another significant figure is Vimalakirti: According to Buddhist lore, he remained a householder with family, yet was so deeply awakened that he revealed the remaining blind spots of bodhisattvas and leading disciples of the Buddha. His emphasis on "being fully engaged in the affairs of an ordinary person without abandoning the dharma" clearly foreshadows Layman P'ang. The Mahayana sutra that tells the story even bears the name of this revered Indian layman. (Mahayana Buddhism, from which the Zen tradition emerged, can be credited with a major shift in focus from monastic to lay practice.)

In the Chinese tradition, around the year 671, Huineng, an illiterate layman who had formerly supported his mother by selling firewood, became the Sixth Patriarch of Zen. This dramatic transmission occurred in the context of a midnight meeting with the Fifth Patriarch in which Hui-neng received the dharma-sanction and Bodhidharma's robe and bowl. Hui-neng then departed, with angry monks chasing after him, for he was but an unlettered layman. Only about five years after this did Huineng have his head shaved and take formal vows.

About one century later, the subject of the present study, Layman P'ang, did not. Why?

The virtues of true renunciation are boundless. So are the vices that self brings to monastic and priestly life. The problems have been there since the beginning, and they persist today. Layman P'ang's decision not to wear the black robe of the Buddhist monk and instead to continue wearing the white clothing of a layman was a virtual watershed for lay Buddhism. It ushered in a tradition that continues to this day of lay Buddhism that is not simply subservient to monks who have "left home" and thus are assumed to be "on the Way." Layman P'ang and his family pioneered a lay Buddhism that is itself the Way.

"Ordinary mind is the Way." This is one of the most famous formulations of Chinese Zen. In other words, all of our daily thoughts and deeds, "collecting firewood and carrying water"—without self-entanglement—are the very dharma we seek. No need for exalted states of mind or exalted robes; the "extraordinarily ordinary" is quite enough.

"Ordinary mind is the Way." The expression was first used by Ma-tsu. His renowned disciple Nan-ch'uan (Jpn.: Nansen) made it famous. Layman P'ang brought it home. Layman P'ang's decision to remain a layman has been lauded for well over a millennium. The P'ang family has become an exemplar of living Buddhism truly "at home," yet unconsumed by material or spiritual possessions.

Let us not forget, however, that it was the monk Shih-t'ou who asked the Layman the question: "So, are you going to wear black or white?" (Dialogue 2) Many of these anecdotes take up the notion of monastic versus lay life. To give just two examples, where the Layman's cap (a sort of head-scarf) comes into play: Layman P'ang's old friend Master Tan-hsia pulls off the Layman's cap and declares, "You look just like an old master to me." The Layman takes it back and places it on Tan-hsia's head with the words, "And you look just like a young coolie to me." What could Tan-hsia do but concur with a, "Yes sir!" (Dialogue 16).

On another occasion, Tse-ch'uan states, "Even though you may prevail, you'd still be wearing that silly head scarf." The Layman takes it off and responds, "Now I look just like the teacher." What could "the teacher" do but laugh out loud? (Dialogue 38)

These playful encounters are compelling precisely because they are done in all seriousness. To take them as mere slapstick is to miss the point. They are stunning illustrations of dharma-at-play—of no-self awakening and compassion working anytime, anywhere. P'ang was a layman, but he was a consummate master of this "play," often giving renowned monks and masters a taste of their own medicine.

Who is this guy? Zen texts tend to be brief when it comes to biographies in general, and thus little detail is given about Layman P'ang's life. We must read between the lines and fill in the necessary details from our own experience. Dialogue 1 states that Layman P'ang "became concerned about the nature of the human condition and sought to understand the reality of it." In other words, he was no different from you or me. For decades as a family man he practiced Buddhism diligently. Eventually he went in search of the leading Zen masters of the time. Encountering Shih-t'ou, he asked, "What about someone who has no connection with the ten thousand dharmas [i.e., all things within and without]?" A word game? An intellectual puzzle? Or perhaps the one and only question remaining for Layman P'ang after long years of intense practice as a householder?

Who, after all, is the one remaining free, unattached to anything? Where is this one in our daily actions, confusions, ups and downs? Isn't this an essential question we all need to be clear about? Is there a more crucial question for us today?

Genuine religious seekers such as Layman P'ang often have a burning question, a great doubt that drives them beyond self: What is the source of suffering? Who am I? What is Bright Virtue? Who is the one not attached to anything?

In the Layman's question can you discern self-entanglement at the end of its rope? Shih-t'ou did. Thus he adroitly placed his hand over P'ang's mouth (Dialogue 1). With this wordless yet most eloquent "answer" Layman P'ang is undone, catching a glimpse of what lies beyond self. (This is the same Shih-t'ou who, when asked by a monk about liberation, replied: "Who binds you!")

The Layman stayed for a time with Shih-t'ou, then went to see Ma-tsu. Does P'ang recount his experiences with Shih-t'ou, does he mention his decision to remain a layman? Perhaps. But all *The Sayings of Layman P'ang* hands down to us is the question he asked. The very same one: "What about someone who has no connection with the ten thousand dharmas?"

With Ma-tsu's response the Layman's final knot comes undone: "I will tell you after you have drunk down the waters of the Yang-tze in one gulp." In other words: "Swallow the universe, then you'll know!"

The Layman's question—and Ma-tsu's answer—soon became famous in Zen circles. Master Chao-chou (Jpn.: Joshu), who was about thirty years of age when the Layman passed away, was later asked the same question. He responded, "Not a person."

In the few other exchanges between the Layman and Ma-tsu recorded here, the Layman continues plugging away, resolving remaining doubts. For example: "How is it that water has neither bone nor muscle, yet is able to hold up a big barge? What is the underlying principle?" He is not asking about shipbuilding or the physical properties of water. And Ma-tsu continues pulling the plug: "For my part there is neither water nor boat. So, what is this bone and muscle you speak of?"

Some time later, when his work with Ma-tsu was done, the Layman visited Master Yueh-shan at his monastery. When the Layman departed, the Master sent a group of new monks to see him off at the gate. The Japanese Zen master Hakuin mentions that this shows Yueh-shan's high regard for Layman P'ang, that he honored him like a great master. It was also a precious opportunity for the monks. It happened to be snowing. The Layman points at the falling snow and exclaims: "The snow is so beautiful, each flake lands in the same place." What is he saying to these recent arrivals accompanying him to the edge of the temple grounds? To rephrase it: "What wondrous snow— each flake falling into place." With self-delusion—that is, the delusion of an independently existing self—gone, each and every thing falls into place of its own accord.

One of the monks asks, "Where do they fall?"—and the Layman slaps him. I will leave the rest of this enchanting exchange (Dialogue 7) in your hands. Here instead is a comment on it from case 42 of the koan collection known as the *Blue Cliff Record*: "As soon as [Layman P'ang] opened his mouth, I'd have just made a snowball and pelted him with it!"

Such critique is actually profound praise, and much more. Keeping the tradition on its toes, vital and alive.

A number of formal koans were eventually culled from Layman P'ang anecdotes, specifically from Dialogues 1, 3, 4, 7, 19, 35, 53, and 55. How did this koan tradition develop, and how is it related to these earlier, spontaneous encounters? Very simply, the Zen tradition holds that the early patriarchs and masters were religious seekers of the highest caliber; they already were primed and ready, so that a brief statement or even just a gesture was enough to evoke realization. An excellent example is the exchange between Bodhidharma and Hui-k'o (Jpn.: Eka), who became the Second Patriarch of Chinese Zen. This encounter constitutes the beginning of the Chinese Zen tradition and is thus foundational (see case 41 of Zenkei Shibayama's *The Gateless Barrier* [Shambhala, 2000]).

Whatever the historical facts, Layman P'ang's encounters with Shih-t'ou and Ma-tsu presented here follow the same pattern. The Layman already had his living koan, that is, his religious problem, burning doubt, ultimate challenge. Such koans have been called *genjo-koan,* the koans manifest right here and now. They spontaneously—inevitably—emerge, often from organic encounters. And they lead to resolute inquiry into the nature of self, that is, to the great matter of birth-and-death: "What about someone who has no connection with the ten thousand dharmas?"

Eventually Zen became more or less the state religion. In the Sung dynasty people from all walks of life were visiting Zen masters. Even if they had a sincere interest, their own religious doubt tended to be vague and unfocused. So, according to the Zen tradition, out of great compassion the masters offered earlier, spontaneous encounters now as set koan cases to help them plumb the depths, or to test their realization. Masters also commented on these encounters, offering their own answer when one was not given, or their alternative answer when one had been given.

Consider Dialogues 33 and 57. The latter, though culled from another source, has the Layman being asked the point of Bodhidharma's coming from the West. This question was becoming part of the lingua franca in Zen circles, a set way of inquiring into the ultimate truth of the Zen teaching. The Layman's laconic response: "Does anyone remember it?" When Ma-tsu was asked the same question, he responded: "Right now what's the point [in asking]?" They actually "answered" the question so exquisitely that it may sound as though they evaded it altogether.

Eventually an elaborate body of prose—and poetic—commentary on koans developed, of which the *Blue Cliff Record* is an outstanding example. Religious verse goes back well before the Buddhist tradition. The earliest Buddhist accounts contain much poetry; the *Thera-gathas* and *Theri-gathas*, verses of the elder monks and nuns, are fine examples of this genre in early Buddhism. The *Sayings of Layman P'ang* presents several of his poems, some of which seem to have been composed on the spot at decisive points in his life. Poetry is a natural form of religious expression, particularly suited to the subject; and it became particularly prominent in Chinese Buddhism, with its rich literary tradition. The statement attributed to Bodhidharma,

"Not relying on words and letters," comes from a four-line poem in classical Chinese.

The use of koan cases developed over the centuries, culminating in the curricula used today in Rinzai monasteries in Japan. The present systems go back around two hundred years. Layman P'ang well reminds us, however, that what we need most is to rouse our own, *living* koan and see it through to the end—whether we're in a monastery or not.

The essential point is not lay or monastic. Layman P'ang was no more attached to lay life than he was to a monastic or priestly one. His life is a revelation of the basic Buddhist truth that, whoever we are and whatever our station, there is finally only one thing to renounce: self. This is no more accomplished through shaving one's head, changing clothes, and taking vows than it is lost in living a family life, making bamboo utensils, and visiting friends.

The difficulties and demands of our lay life, however, are real and need to be faced. The layman's sacrifices, and those of his spouse and children, are not described in the text. We must fill in those details, with utmost care, from our own experience.

Gotama Buddha's sacrifice for the liberation of all beings is worthy of veneration. But what about renouncing one's family in order to seek the Way? That was not the way for Vimalakirti, nor for Layman P'ang. Nor is it the way for us today.

It bears repeating: The real question is not about being lay *or* monastic. It is about awakening to no-self and living in the world with compassion. To the extent that living a monastic or priestly life actually creates such conditions, it is a path worthy of respect. Just as a layperson's life is.

The contributions of laypeople throughout Buddhist history have been enormous. Early Buddhism would probably not have survived without lay support. Much great Zen culture was created by laypeople rather than by Zen monks or priests. Just to give a few outstanding examples: the poetry, painting, and calligraphy of Wang Wei, the calligraphy and poetry of Su Tung-p'o, the painting of Liang-k'ai, Hasegawa Tohaku, and Miyamoto (Musashi) Niten, and the tea utensils such as the bamboo flower containers of Kobori Enshu.

To what extent was Layman P'ang inspired by the enlightened layperson tradition, and to what extent did he and his family help to create it? It is hard to say. Either way, the *Sayings of Layman P'ang* is the only Zen classic featuring a layperson. It provides a precious human image, especially for our modern, secular society. An unerring beacon for what we aspire to, and for what we truly are: in leaving no trace of self, we are fully involved in the work of the world.

It remains to be seen whether or not the precious monastic component of Zen will succeed outside Asia.

Genuine monastic training is precious indeed. Layman P'ang, when his time was ripe, appears to have spent a good deal of time in monasteries. Today as well, for those who really want to get their toes wet, at least several months or years of practice in an authentic Zen monastery is strongly recommended.

In the modern world, however, lay Zen will naturally be the focus. It is just a matter of time until a real lay Zen springs forth among ordinary folks with ordinary minds, amidst householders around the globe. Indeed, the initial cultivation is already well underway.

Zen Buddhist retreats for laypeople in the West have been growing in frequency and numbers in recent years. Lay retreats have been held in Europe and the United States, blazing an authentic Zen path on home ground in the modern world, providing opportunities for real encounters with elder sisters and brothers in the dharma. Layman P'ang's descendants are everywhere.

Buddhism's fundamental goal has been described in the Pali canon as the cessation of this whole mass of suffering entangled in the grand "I am" conceit. The Layman expressed it this way in two stanzas of a poem (Dialogue 52):

> The will to survive must be killed off,
> Once it is killed off, there will be peace. . . .
>
> Aren't the esteemed sages
> Just regular people who've resolved this matter?

Whether you slowly savor each dialogue or gulp it down, I trust the Layman's marvelous medicine will do its work, and that you will find the place underfoot illumined anew.

Jeff Shore
Tofukuji Training Monastery
Kyoto, 2008

Translator's Note

The idea of making a new translation of *The Sayings of Layman P'ang* arose during discussions I had with Fukushima Roshi in 2002. At that time, it was suggested that I undertake the translation with the acknowledgment that the Zen movement emerging in the West is predominantly a layman's practice rather than a monastic one, as it has traditionally been in Asia. In any case, the translation by Ruth Fuller Sasaki, Yoshitaka Iriya, and Dana R. Fraser had long been out of print and the thought was that, at that time, the text hadn't received the audience it deserves among Zen practitioners, so its reintroduction now might bring greater attention to it.

In this undertaking, I am indebted to Professor Yoshitaka Iriya, not only for presenting the original Chinese text itself—an edition published by Hsi-yin Temple in the tenth year of the Ch'ung-chen period of the Ming dynasty (1637)—but also for his meticulous scholarship in regard to biographical information and textual references. In addition, the project would have been inconceivable without Fukushima Roshi's continual support in helping me understand the subtlety and nuance of Zen expression.

From a technical point of view, I feel that there are two important points to mention about the text that may not be apparent to the first-time reader of a book of Zen anecdotes.

One point is the fact that other texts of this variety—many of the Zen masters of this period (especially the line that runs from Ma-tsu to Lin-chi) *do* have their own books of "recorded sayings"—are usually full of "a monk asked the Master" type of anecdote. These kinds of anecdotes are a little one-sided because they pit the old Zen master against a young monk. In fact, one can almost sense the older monks in the background goading a newcomer to ask the crotchety old master, "Does the puppy have Buddha nature or not?" By contrast, the anecdotes in the *Layman P'ang* text depict two accomplished Zen friends posing "testing questions" to each other in a more organic way.

The other important point about the text that may not be readily evident to the reader is the way that the anecdotes are categorized and presented. All the anecdotes that are relevant to each of the Layman's Zen friends (nearly twenty in all) are grouped together—giving the impression that they all occurred in serial fashion while the Layman was staying at a particular friend's place for a while.

Though in some cases this is true (as with the anecdotes concerning Shih-t'ou, Ma-tsu, and Yueh-shan that occur at the beginning of the text), by and large it is not.

Although there is only one anecdote associated with some of the personalities that appear in the text, it is generally the case that there are multiple anecdotes associated with each of them. Rather than being construed as occurring in serial fashion, these anecdotes should be understood as separate occasions spread out over a long period. The Layman was a free spirit and frequently came to visit one or another of these Zen friends who were living in the hills of Hunan Province at the time. Furthermore, it should also be acknowledged that the anecdotes assembled here do *not* represent *all* of the Layman's visits with any of the Zen friends depicted: Not every visit yielded a memorable anecdote. Thus, in spite of the way that the text is organized, the Layman should be seen as trekking freely around the hills where he lived, dropping in on one or another of his Zen friends quite regularly. That his Zen friends did the same can be inferred from the text, but the Layman (since he was a layman, and so not responsible for maintaining residence at a temple) was much freer to do so than they were.

I would also like to mention here some of the other "housekeeping" details involved in the translation. One is of course the phonetic rendering of Chinese. Although pinyin phonetics for the most part give a clearer representation of how the written word is pronounced in Chinese,

I have adhered to the Wade-Giles phonetic system to render the Chinese names in this text. I feel it still has some legitimacy in translating the old texts, and it is the system I was trained in.

Furthermore, even though it is through the Japanese tradition that most Western practitioners are familiar with the names of many Zen personalities, those who appear in the text are Chinese, so I have used their Chinese names throughout, giving their Japanese equivalents only on first mention.

A word should be said about the process of translation itself, particularly regarding how much interpretation is involved in the process. Old texts written in classical Chinese, as the T'ang dynasty Zen texts are, can leave a lot to the imagination of the translator. Thus, it is almost inevitable that different versions will vary stylistically. A translator's task is to understand the meaning of words, phrases, and passages in the original language and render them into a different language in a way that not only preserves that meaning but also retains the flavor of the original vocabulary and phrasing. Naturally, reconciling these two is not always a simple feat, so variations in renderings occur. To maintain a middle path in this endeavor is every translator's intention. In this regard, I hope my rendering of the text is transparent to the underlying meaning, yet preserves the flavor of the original language as well.

Acknowledgments

In making this translation, I have received assistance from a number of people, whom I'd like to thank.

Naturally, without Fukushima Roshi's patient instruction over the years, this project would have been inconceivable. Similarly, my Dharma coworkers Tayo Gabler, Hap Tivey, Hisashi Miura, and Jeff Shore have been a source of continuing inspiration. In addition, I bow to George Winiarski and Naomi Rubine, whose door has always been open to a weary traveler, and San Albers, whose resourcefulness and technical assistance have been invaluable. Finally, a special thanks to my old friend Michael Hofmann, not only for the paintings that bring the text to life, but for the good times we've shared.

The Recorded Sayings of Layman P'ang
compiled by Imperial Commissioner Yu Ti

Prologue

The Layman's given name was Yun (Un), but he was known as Tao-hsuan (Dogen).[1] Although he was born in the town of Hsiang-yang,[2] he lived in the city of Heng-yang[3] where his father was employed by the governor.[4]

At the family residence in the southern part of the city, there was a cottage near the main house where they practiced meditation. For many years the Layman's whole family practiced the Way.[5] The cottage was called Wu-k'ung Cottage (Goku-an).[6] Later, the property was given away to be used as a temple rather than a residence, and was renamed Neng-jen Temple (Nojin-ji).

At the beginning of the Chen-yuan period,[7] the family's valuables, worth an untold amount, were transported by boat up the Hsiang River[8] to the right side of Lake Tung-t'ing. There the boat was scuttled.[9] After this, the family's existence was hand to mouth. The Layman and his wife, with their son and daughter, labored together morning and night making bamboo utensils and selling them in the market.

In the Chen-yuan period, the Zen teaching was being established with great vigor and the teachings of the Masters was a common topic of conversation.[10] Thus, like rays of light, it multiplied and spread out, finding its way everywhere.

The Layman first went to practice at Shih-t'ou's place, where all barriers suddenly melted away for him. Later, he went to see Ma-tsu and delved deeper into his fundamental consciousness.[11] Conflicts merged into unity and everything was in accordance with the Way. His profound eloquence, like that of Manjushri,[12] formed a complete circle with his actual demonstrations. This is amply recounted in various historical records that are in ever-wider circulation.

At the beginning of the Yuan-he period,[13] the Layman camped out on a cliff in the vicinity of Hsiang-yang. The place was twelve miles south of Mount Lu-men[14] and is now called Layman's Rock.

At the time, Duke Yu,[15] the governor, had sent out his representatives among the people to survey their sentiments [listen to their songs], and a small collection of the Layman's poems came into their hands. When Duke Yu read it he was filled with admiration for its unique quality. He waited for an opportune time and subsequently went in person to meet the Layman. From their first meeting, it was as if they were old friends. They clearly understood each other's spirit, and Duke Yu came and went continually.

When the Layman was on his deathbed, he called his daughter, Ling-chao, to him and told her, "The world of appearances has no substance other than that which you give to it. If you observe how day becomes night, can it be said when it has reached halfway [is noon]?"

Ling-chao went outside and told him, "It is daytime, yet there is some obscurity. Can you clear it up for me?"

The Layman said, "That's how it is!"

Ling-chao said, "That's how it is!"

The Layman got out of bed and looked out the window. Ling-chao was meditating on a bench when she suddenly vanished. The Layman looked around to see where she had gone, then laughed, saying, "My girl has fitted the arrowhead to the shaft."

Then he dampened the fire and put the house in order.

After a week had passed, the Duke came to pay his respects. The Layman laid his hand in the Duke's lap, fixed his gaze on the eternal, and recited a verse:

Our hollow desires,
Comprise what is something [form].
The awareness that has no substance,
Comprises what is nothing [emptiness].
A good day in the world
Is but a side effect.

After he finished the verse, a strange fragrance filled the room, and the Layman sat up in meditation and composed his mind. The Duke cried out in lament, and after a long time had passed, he left.

> A sudden gust of wind from a distant land
> Silences the incessant sounds of nature.
> As the moon advances to its last phase,
> On the waves its golden light is extinguished.[16]

Just as in the old saying "The rivers and lakes will eventually evaporate," the funeral ceremonies were entirely an example of "letting things go."[17]

Eventually, news of the Layman's death reached his wife. Upon hearing of it she said, "My crazy daughter and the blockhead Chinaman have gone without consulting me.[18] How can I put up with this?"

Subsequently, she went to inform her son.[19] Finding him in the fields burning the straw from the rice harvest, she told him, "Mr. P'ang and Ling-chao are gone."

Hearing this, the son dropped his hoe, shouted, "Oh no!" and passed away right where he was standing.

The Layman's wife said, "If my crazy son is so foolish, why should I alone remain?" Later, there was a cremation.

People thought this was extraordinary. Soon after, Mrs. P'ang spread the word of what happened throughout her village, then went away. Although afterward people went to locate her, no matter how hard they looked, no one was ever able to find her.

The Layman once said:

The world over,
Men without wives,
Women lacking husbands,
Face to face,
Speaking of what is unborn.[20]

This is a verse that addresses the mystery of the Way. It has been discussed for many generations, but very few have gotten the point.

The text that I have been talking about has been published in an edition of two volumes with the hope that it will be instructive to those of coming generations.

The Layman is widely regarded as a present-day Vimalakirti.[21] This is quite apt.

Contributed by a nameless person.[22]

---

1. Though Tao-hsuan was not formally a dharma name inasmuch as the Layman never became a monk, it functions in much the same way and has the "ring" of a dharma name.

2. Hsiang-yang was an important city in the province of present-day Hubei and is now known as Xiangfan.

3. Heng-yang is a large city about three hundred miles south of Hsiang-yang in present-day Hunan Province.

4. It is unclear in the text whether the Layman's father *was* the governor of Heng-yang or employed by the governor. Professor Iriya notes that in the Later Han period a certain Duke P'ang-te is recorded as having been the governor of Heng-yang. That this Duke P'ang-te is an ancestor of the Layman is quite probable, but whether or not his father was governor is not clearly established.

5. The Way is the Buddhist path to enlightenment.

6. Wu-k'ung translates as "awakening to emptiness." The existence of the Neng-jen Temple is noted—and so its historical significance is verified—by public records as recently as the eighteenth century.

7. The Chen-yuan period of the T'ang dynasty ran from 785 to 805.

8. A large river and tributary of the West River that runs through Hunan Province.

9. The text is ambiguous as to what really happened—whether the boat was sunk, whether the valuables were thrown overboard, or whether they were hidden and later washed away in a flood—but the traditional interpretation is that the boat was sunk. There is only speculation as to why the Layman decided to pack off the family wealth, since T'ang China was fairly stable politically at this time. The traditional view has him wanting to scale back the opulence of his surroundings to be more in accordance with the Zen penchant for simplicity, and many references to the Layman's exemplary renunciation of wealth exist in Zen literature.

10. The great Zen master Ma-tsu Tao-i (Baso Doitsu) is traditionally credited for the burgeoning of interest in Zen at this time. That he lived relatively nearby forms part of the historical underpinning for the Layman's attraction to Zen.

11. This term—"fundamental consciousness"—is usually translated as "original mind," and indeed this phrasing can be construed as implying that Ma-tsu gave the Layman his sanction.

12. Manjushri is the Bodhisattva of Wisdom in the Buddhist tradition. He appears in both the *Lotus Sutra* and the *Avatamsaka Sutra.*

13. The Yuan-he period of the T'ang dynasty ran from 806 to 821.

14. The character here for "mountain" could refer to an actual mountain, or it could refer to the Lu-men (Deer Gate) Temple that Mrs. P'ang is recorded to have visited in anecdote 58. It has become Zen custom to refer to Zen temples as "mountains" whether they are actually sited on mountains or not. In any case, the temple and mountain can be assumed to have close proximity to each other. Lu-men Temple is referred to in a poem by the poet Meng Hao-jan who lived in the generation before the Layman and was also a native of Hsiang-yang. We are not told *why* the Layman decided to move back to the vicinity of Hsiang-yang.

15. Duke Yu is considered to be the person responsible for the original edition of *The Sayings of Layman P'ang.* He is documented as a capable but ruthless administrator who strictly persecuted mendicant Buddhist monks in his domain until he was "enlightened" during a famous encounter with the Zen priest Tsu-yu (Shigyoku). One other point that should be touched on briefly here is that this text differs from others of its kind from the period in that it was not compiled by the immediate disciples of the Zen master whose teachings are presented. Indeed, in the Layman's case there were no disciples. The original T'ang-dynasty text was compiled by Duke Yu, who, as is documented in the Prologue,

became a close friend of the Layman in the two years preceding his death. It must be presumed that, using the powers of his office, Duke Yu collected these anecdotes by sending his minions around the countryside to inquire about the Layman's contacts with the Zen friends we meet in the text. Though it is difficult to determine when the text first appeared, the anecdotes contained in it are referred to in Sung-dynasty texts that have come down to us. Not long after the Layman's death, Duke Yu was promoted from governor of Hsiang-yang to the rank of Imperial Commissioner.

16. This verse of eulogy is not attributed, though it is thought to be one of the Layman's poems. As an interesting sidebar, Professor Iriya points out that the original text of the *Layman P'ang* is referred to in many early sources as having contained three hundred poems, most of which have been lost over the centuries. What is interesting is that Professor Iriya—who had published a work on the poems of Han-shan (Kanzan) prior to his work on the *Layman P'ang* text (and, in fact, assisted Burton Watson in his English-language version [Columbia University Press, 1971])—surmises that, due to similarity in style and content, the "lost" poems could be what is now considered to be the work of "Han-shan." Layman P'ang and Han-shan would have been contemporaries, both having lived during the latter half of the eighth century to the beginning of the ninth century. Layman P'ang, however, lived in Hunan Province, while Han-shan is said to have lived on Mount T'ien-tai—south of Hangzhou in present-day Zhejiang Province—quite a long distance away, especially in those days. In any case, there is no evidence one way or the other on this issue.

17. "Letting things go" is literally "tying them to rushes."

18. "Chinaman" here means a common, uneducated person, a "peasant."

19. Although the Layman's wife is mentioned once in the text itself, his son is only mentioned here in the Prologue.

20. See anecdote 3 in the Dialogues with Ma-tsu.

21. See anecdote 36, note 2, on Vimalakirti.

22. The writer of the Prologue does not identify himself, but it can be understood that he is a Zen priest and/or possibly the person who sponsored the copying and republication of this text. Though this translation was made using an original woodblock edition that dates from the tenth year of the Ch'ung-cheng period of the Ming dynasty (1637), this same Prologue is included in a Japanese transcription of a Sung-dynasty text done in the mid-fifteenth century.

1. Suddenly Stopping the World

The Layman named P'ang-yun (Ho-un) lived in the city of Heng-yang but was born in the province of Hsiang. He was known as Tao-hsuan (Dogen). In his youth, he was a Confucian scholar who became concerned about the nature of the human condition and sought to understand the reality of it.

In the first year of the Chen-yuan period,[1] the Layman went to see Zen Master Shih-t'ou[2] and asked him, "What about someone who has no connection with the ten thousand *dharmas*?"[3]

Shih-t'ou put his hand over the Layman's mouth, and the Layman had a sudden realization.

---

1. The year 785.

2. Shih-t'ou Hsi-ch'ien (Sekito Kisen, 700–790) was a dharma heir of Ch'ing-yuan Hsing-szu (Seigen Gyoshi, 660–740),

who was one of the three main disciples of the Sixth Patriarch. Shih-t'ou was one of the most renowned Zen masters
of the T'ang dynasty. The Soto lineage of Zen practiced in
Japan is ultimately traceable to him. He lived on Mount
Nam-yueh (also called Heng-shan or Mount Heng), to the
north of the Layman's hometown of Heng-yang.

3. Whereas "The Dharma" is the Truth, or Buddha's teaching,
the "ten thousand dharmas" are "all worldly phenomena."

2. Subtleties of Daily Life

One day Shih-t'ou said, "I've come to visit you. What have you been doing?"

The Layman said, "If you're asking what I do every day, there's nothing to say about it."

Shih-t'ou said, "What did you think you were doing before I asked you about it?"

The Layman made up a verse:

What I do every day
Is nothing special:
I simply stumble around.
What I do is not thought out,
Where I go is unplanned.
No matter who tries to leave their mark,
The hills and dales are not impressed.
Collecting firewood and carrying water
Are prayers that reach the gods.

Shih-t'ou approved, saying, "So, are you going to wear black or white?[1]

The Layman said, "I will do whatever is best."

It came to pass that he never shaved his head to join the sangha.

---

1. Black robes were worn by monks, and white robes were worn by laypeople.

3. One Gulp

Afterward, the Layman went to Chiang-hsi to study with Ma-tsu[1] and asked him, "What about someone who has no connection with the ten thousand *dharmas*?"

Ma-tsu said, "I will tell you after you have drunk down the waters of the West River in one gulp."

The Layman understood the deep meaning implied, and composed a verse:

> With an empty mind
> The examination is passed.[2]

After he'd stayed with the Master for two years, he composed a verse:

> The world over:
> Men without wives,
> Women without husbands;

Face to face,
Speaking of what is unborn.[3]

---

1. Ma-tsu Tao-i (709–788) lived in present-day Jiangxi Province, which borders Hunan to the east. Ma-tsu was a dharma heir of Nan-yueh Huai-jang (Nangaku Ejo, 677–744), who was also one of the three main disciples of the Sixth Patriarch. Ma-tsu is considered to be a pivotal figure in Zen history because of the number of monks who came to study with him and the number of dharma heirs he sanctioned (said to be over one hundred). He is credited with helping to popularize Zen in China during the T'ang dynasty, and the Rinzai lineage of Zen practiced in Japan is ultimately traceable to him.

2. This is a reference to the Mandarin exams that the Layman had once set out to take with Tan-hsia, but never did (see chapter 12, note 1, regarding Tan-hsia). In other sources (the "Ancestors' Hall Collection") a fuller version is given for this verse:

> Coming to this place from all directions,
> They all study nondoing (wu-wei).
> But right here where Buddhas are selected,
> The examination is passed with an empty mind.

3. The Layman is considered to be in the lineage of Ma-tsu because the deepening of his Zen experience (as reflected in this anecdote) occurred while he studied with him. In most "genealogical trees" of the Zen heritage, the Layman is

listed as one of the twelve main dharma heirs of Ma-tsu. When the laymen practiced with him, Ma-tsu was in his late seventies and in the last years of his life. Since the time given for the Layman's stays with Shih-t'ou and Ma-tsu, after 785, is relatively close to the date of Ma-tsu's death, it can be assumed that the Layman began practicing on his own shortly after Ma-tsu's death when the Layman was probably in his mid-forties.

4. A Distinctly Authentic Person

At another time, the Layman asked Ma-tsu, "If you met someone who was a distinctly authentic person, how would you recognize him?"

Ma-tsu directed his gaze downward.

The Layman said, "Only you are able to play a tune on a stringless harp."

Ma-tsu looked up and the Layman bowed. Ma-tsu then returned to his room. The Layman followed him, saying, "Just now, I tried to trick you, but you made a fool out of me instead."

5. The Bone and Muscle of Water

One day the Layman asked Ma-tsu, "How is it that water has neither bone nor muscle, yet is able to hold up a big barge? What is the underlying principle?"

Ma-tsu said, "For my part there is neither water nor boat. So, what is this bone and muscle you speak of?"

6. One Vehicle

When the Layman arrived at Yueh-shan's[1] place, Yueh-shan asked him, "Were you able to come all the way here by one vehicle?"[2]

The Layman said, "Although I was advised to choose an auspicious day to meet you, I have no idea how far I've come."

Yueh-shan said, "The Layman has seen Shih-t'ou, has he not?"

The Layman said, "Shih-t'ou was never very crafty about revealing something or withholding something."[3]

Yueh-shan said, "If you will excuse me, this old abbot has some business to attend to."

As the Layman was preparing to leave, Yueh-shan said, "Actually, he was very crafty at revealing something or withholding something."

The Layman said, "Yes, but that craft was lost today in your question about the one vehicle of our heritage."

Yueh-shan said, "So it was; so it was."

1. Yueh-shan Wei-yen (Yakusan Igen, 745–828) studied with both Ma-tsu and Shih-t'ou, but he is considered to be one of Shih-t'ou's dharma heirs. Yueh-shan was a native of Shan-hsi (present-day Shanxi) Province, where the T'ang capital of Ch'ang-an (Xi'an) is located, but his temple was in Hunan Province to the west of Lake Tung-t'ing. Yueh-shan is also a progenitor of the Soto lineage of Zen as the "grandfather" of Tung-shan Liang-chieh (Tozan Ryokai).

2. The "one vehicle" is a reference to Shih-t'ou's teaching—which is, of course, the expression of the entire Zen lineage—as well as a reference to the fact that though both Yueh-shan and the Layman studied with Shih-t'ou, they are each now on their own.

3. This is a reference to a Zen master's teaching techniques.

7. Viewing the Snow

When the Layman decided to leave Yueh-shan's temple,[1] Yueh-shan instructed ten novice monks to escort him to the front gate. At that time, the Layman pointed to the falling snow and said, "The snow is so beautiful; each flake lands in the same place."

One among the group of monks asked, "Where do they fall?"

The Layman slapped him.

Another of the monks said, "Aren't you being a bit cheeky?"

The Layman said, "What about you? Calling yourself a novice monk when Satan still has a hold on you."

The monk said, "What do you mean?"

The Layman slapped him also, and said, "Looking but not seeing; speaking but saying nothing."

1. It is unclear from the text how long the Layman stayed at Yueh-shan's monastery, but it seems fair to assume that he didn't stay that long—certainly not years.

8. There You Are

When the Layman arrived at Ch'i-feng's[1] place, he had only just entered the temple grounds when Ch'i-feng said, "The outsider[2] enters the temple grounds so furtively. What could he be looking for?"

The Layman looked all around and said, "Is someone speaking to me? Is someone speaking to me?"

Ch'i-feng laughed, and the Layman said, "Oh, there you are!"

Ch'i-feng said, "I haven't said a word!"

The Layman said, "Then someone must be talking behind your back."

Ch'i-feng looked behind him and said, "Look! Look! [There he goes!]"[3]

The Layman said, "The clever thief has made off with everything! The clever thief has made off with everything!"

Ch'i-feng did not reply.

1. Ch'i-feng was one of the dharma heirs of Ma-tsu. Other than these anecdotes in the *Layman P'ang*, nothing has been passed down about him.
2. The term refers to someone who is not a member of the Buddhist sangha.
3. He is suggesting some (unseen) person is running away.

9. Front and Rear

One day when Ch'i-feng and the Layman had gone out for a walk, the Layman was a step ahead of Ch'i-feng and he said, "As I am a step ahead, I must be stronger than the teacher."

Ch'i-feng said, "It's not that I'm behind; it's just that senior citizens are allowed to go first."

The Layman said, "When someone has an affliction, it is not polite to mention their affliction."

Ch'i-feng said, "I'm afraid you're not content in your old age!"

The Layman said, "If I were not content about the afflictions of old age, what would you do to give me relief?"

Ch'i-feng said, "If I had a stick handy, I'd beat you until my arm hurt."

The Layman slapped Ch'i-feng, saying, "Just a small beating would do."

Ch'i-feng picked up a stick, but the Layman grabbed it from him and said, "Right here and right now, the thief has been robbed blind."

Ch'i-feng laughed and said, "Is it that I'm so dull, or that you are so sharp?"

The Layman clapped his hands and said, "Even-steven, even-steven."

10. The Distance to the Mountaintop

On another day, the Layman asked Ch'i-feng, "Do you know how far it is from here to the top of the peak?"[1]

Ch'i-feng said, "I'm not sure if you can really get there from here."

The Layman said, "If it were so awfully steep and treacherous, I wouldn't have asked about it."

Ch'i-feng said, "You tell me how far it is, then."

The Layman said, "One, two, three . . ."

Ch'i-feng said, "Four, five, six . . ."

The Layman said, "Why not 'seven'?"

Ch'i-feng said, "You say 'seven,' then I'll say 'eight.'"

The Layman said, "You've made it [to the top]."

Ch'i-feng said, "I've finally amounted to something!"

The Layman and Ch'i-feng both laughed and then went for a walk together.

1. This is a play upon Ch'i-feng's name, which means "reach-
   ing the pinnacle."

11. That Which Is Not Spoken

On another day, the Layman asked, "Will you not tell me something about what is at hand?"[1]

Ch'i-feng said, "I will, as soon as that old codger Mr. P'ang gets here."

The Layman said, "Aren't you up to it today?"

Ch'i-feng said, "That's a good question, but why are you asking me?"

The Layman said, "Well done! Well done!"

---

1. This is a difficult term to translate; it has the meaning of something that is "clear and present."

12. Meeting Ling-chao

One day, Master Tan-hsia T'ien-jan (Tanka Tennen)[1] came to visit the Layman. He had just passed through the gate when he saw the Layman's daughter, Ling-chao, holding a basket of vegetables.

Tan-hsia said, "Is the Layman here or not?"

Ling-chao dropped the basket, stood up, and clasped her hands together on her chest.[2]

Tan-hsia again asked, "Is the Layman here or not?"

Ling-chao picked up the basket and walked away, and Tan-hsia left.

When the Layman returned home, Ling-chao told him what had happened.

The Layman said, "Was it Tan-hsia?"

Ling-chao said, "He's gone now."

The Layman said, "You've spilled the milk in the mud."[3]

1. Tan-hsia T'ien-jan (739–823) was one of the four principal
dharma heirs of Shih-t'ou and was a friend of the Layman's
when they were young men. It is reported in other sources
(most notably the Ancestors' Hall Collection) that at some
point in his youth the Layman became acquainted with Tan-
hsia, and they went to Chang-an to study for the Mandarin
exams together. At some point in their journey, they decided
to change course and visited Ma-tsu's monastery. From this
we can infer that, though his birth date is not given in the
text, the Layman was near the same age as Tan-hsia, who was
born in 739. Although they started on the Zen path together,
they eventually went their separate ways. Tan-hsia joined the
sangha, while the Layman did not. Tan-hsia was known as
T'ien-jan, "the Natural"—a nickname reportedly given to
him by Ma-tsu. Well known for his unconventional Zen
style, Tan-hsia appears in a famous anecdote burning a
wooden Buddha image to keep warm in the winter:

> One freezing cold day in winter, Tan-hsia took the
> wooden Buddha statue from the altar in the temple
> where he was staying and used it to make a fire. By
> chance, the resident priest came along and saw him.
> "How can you burn up my wooden Buddha?" he
> asked.
>
> Tan-hsia poked the coals with his staff and said,
> "I'm burning it to get at the sacred remains." [The
> "sacred remains" refer to the bits of bone that were
> left after the Buddha's body was cremated.]
>
> The resident priest said, "How can there be any
> sacred remains in a wooden Buddha?"

Tan-hsia replied, "If not, let's burn the two attendant statues as well."

At this, the resident priest's eyebrows fell out. [This is a Zen metaphor meaning his lack of true understanding was revealed.]

After Shih-t'ou's death in 790, Tan-hsia wandered around the country for many years before settling at Mount Tan-hsia in Henan Province toward the end of his life, when he was eighty-one. (He took his "master's name" from the place where his temple was located, as was the Zen custom in those days.) It is recorded that, four years after settling at the monastery, Tan-hsia declared he was going out on pilgrimage again and died while putting on his sandals for the last time. The anecdotes recorded here apparently occurred during Tan-hsia's wanderings while he stayed in the Layman's neighborhood and depict the time when Tan-hsia and the Layman reestablished their old friendship. Tan-hsia outlived the Layman by almost twenty years.

2. A gesture of greeting in old China.

3. A wasted effort. Layman P'ang is saying that it was unnecessary for Ling-chao to try to test Tan-hsia's Zen.

13. Deaf and Dumb

Afterward, Tan-hsia went to visit the Layman again. When the Layman saw him approaching, he didn't stand up or say anything.

Tan-hsia held up his whisk.[1]

The Layman held up a pestle [that he was holding].

Tan-hsia said, "That's it? Nothing else?"

The Layman said, "Now I see you have become a master. Things are not the same as they were before."[2]

Tan-hsia said, "Don't be prejudiced by appearances."

The Layman said, "But you've already been put to the test once [when you came before]."

Tan-hsia said, "I don't know why I said nothing then."

The Layman said, "It was your right to say nothing. When I am annoyed, I also say nothing."

Tan-hsia lowered his whisk and turned to leave.

The Layman called to him, saying, "Brother Jan! Brother Jan!"[3] but Tan-hsia did not turn around.

The Layman said, "Not only can't you say anything, you also can't hear anything."[4]

---

1. A whisk was one of the standard implements allowed to traveling monks. It was used to clean the ground for meditation. Later, it became more of a ceremonial implement identified with a Zen master.

2. Because now Tan-hsia was wearing the garb of a Zen master.

3. A familiar form of address between Dharma brothers.

4. This passage is extremely difficult to translate in its fullest meaning. There are not only significant nuances that convey the deep friendship and familiarity these two men have with each other, but also subtleties of Zen reference that are perhaps impossible to fully capture. The Layman wants to apologize to his old friend for his daughter's cheeky behavior but also wants to keep it within the context of their Zen understanding rather than revert back to their familiarity of earlier days.

14. The Layman and Mr. P'ang

On another day, Tan-hsia came to visit the Layman. As he entered the gateway they saw each other and Tan-hsia asked, "Is the Layman here or not?"[1]

The Layman said, "He died of starvation while fasting."

Tan-hsia said, "Well, is old man P'ang here or not?"

The Layman said, "Oh my god! Oh my god!" and he went into his house.

Tan-hsia said, "Oh my god! Oh my god!" and left.[2]

---

1. See anecdote 12, in which Tan-hsia uses the same "testing question."

2. This anecdote should be considered as a whole with the two preceding anecdotes in terms of depicting the Layman and Tan-hsia reestablishing the friendship that was interrupted by their differing paths in life.

15. The Eye of the Heritage

One day Tan-hsia asked the Layman, "How is today like yesterday when we met each other?"

The Layman said, "Yesterday we had to quibble about the dharma in order to open the eye of our heritage."

Tan-hsia said, "How would Mr. P'ang know when the eye of our heritage has opened?"

The Layman said, "I see from inside your eye."

Tan-hsia said, "But my eye is so narrow. How can you sequester yourself in there?"

The Layman said, "How can you say that your eye is narrow, or that I can't sequester myself in there?"

Tan-hsia hesitated, so the Layman said, "Can you not say a word that would complete our conversation?"

Tan-hsia again did not reply, and the Layman said, "No one can say it all in a word."

16. The Head Scarf

One day the Layman came while Tan-hsia was in meditation. The Layman stood in front of him and clasped his hands on his chest [in greeting], but Tan-hsia did not look up. After a few minutes, the Layman moved away and took a seat. Tan-hsia then got up and stood in front of the Layman with his hands clasped to his chest. After a few minutes, he turned to go into his room.

The Layman then said, "I come in and you go out. What's the matter?"

Tan-hsia said, "When this old man comes, he comes. When he goes, he goes. There's really nothing to it."

The Layman said, "Don't you have one iota of compassion?"

Tan-hsia said, "This Chinaman just goes along to wherever he is led."

The Layman said, "When you are being led along, what takes hold of you?"

Tan-hsia then pulled off the Layman's head scarf[1] and said, "You look just like an old master to me."

The Layman grabbed his head scarf back and put it on Tan-hsia's head, saying, "And you look just like a young coolie[2] to me."

Tan-hsia said, "Yes sir! Yes sir! Yes sir!"

The Layman said, "So, there is still a little of that old-time spirit left after all."

Tan-hsia took the Layman's head scarf off his head and said, "What a filthy old rag this is!"

The Layman said, "Yes sir! Yes sir! Yes sir!"

Tan-hsia said, "The attempt to maintain the old-time spirit has been long forgotten."

The Layman snapped his fingers three times and said, "Heaven and Earth have changed places!"

---

1. The Layman had a shaved head like a monk. A black head scarf was worn by common laborers.

2. A common laborer.

17. Seven and One

One day, when Tan-hsia saw the Layman coming, he took a step backward.

The Layman said, "What? Have you forgotten yourself? Where is that usual indomitable look?"

Tan-hsia sat down in meditation.

The Layman stood in front of him and wrote the number 7 on the ground with his staff, then wrote the number 7 underneath it, saying, "The seven is seen as one, and when the one is seen, the seven is forgotten."

Tan-hsia then stood up.

The Layman said, "Please sit a while longer and compose a second line for my verse."

Tan-hsia said, "What more can be added to that?"

The Layman then shouted three times and left.

18. Making Waves

One day, the Layman was out for a walk with Tan-hsia when they came upon a deep, clear pond.

The Layman gestured toward it and said, "Consider this![1] Can you devise a way to make use of this?"

Tan-hsia said, "This is obvious! A way to use this can't be devised."

The Layman then splashed the water onto Tan-hsia twice.

Tan-hsia said, "Stop this! Stop this!"

The Layman said, "You asked for this! You asked for this!"

Tan-hsia then splashed the Layman three times, saying, "So, now what else are you going to do with this?"

The Layman said, "There's nothing left to do."

Tan-hsia said, "There aren't many who have such luck."

The Layman said, "Who has had such luck?"[2]

1. The word "this" has a "loaded" meaning in this anecdote: the fullness of reality in the present moment.

2. Other texts have a slightly different rendering of this anecdote, but there are too many variations to include them all here.

19. Potent Instruction

One day the Layman and the priest Pai-ling[1] met each other on the road.

Pai-ling said, "Aren't you the Layman who long ago received some potent instruction[2] from Shih-t'ou[3] that, even now, many monks still quibble over?"

The Layman said, "Are they still quibbling over that?"

Pai-ling said, "Who is all the quibbling about?"

The Layman pointed to himself and said, "Mr. P'ang."

Pai-ling said, "So, then! I have someone right here in front of me who can tell me all about Manjushri and Subhuti,[4] do I?"

The Layman then asked him, "Is the Master someone who has knowledge about this 'potent instruction'?"

Pai-ling put his hat back on and continued on his way.

The Layman said, "Happy trails!"[5] but Pai-ling did not look back.

1. Pai-ling was a disciple of Ma-tsu. Other than these passages in the *Layman P'ang* text, there are no anecdotes about him and nothing else is known of him.

2. This refers to the Layman's initial awakening experience.

3. See anecdote 1, note 2, on pages 13–14 about Shih-t'ou.

4. Manjushri is considered to be the guardian of Buddhist wisdom. Though historically a disciple of the Buddha, he has come to be regarded as a bodhisattva (a kind of demigod). He appears both in the *Lotus Sutra* and the *Avatamsaka Sutra*. Subhuti was also one of the original disciples of the Buddha and is taken as the model of the devoted disciple in Buddhist tradition. He appears in the *Diamond Sutra*.

5. The Chinese phrase translated as "Happy trails" was a standard parting salutation in T'ang times, equal to "Have a good journey."

20. Speaking and Not Speaking

One day Pai-ling asked the Layman, "Both speaking about it and not speaking about it are unavoidable. So can you tell me simply, how do you not avoid speaking about it?"

The Layman winked at him.

Pai-ling said, "Nothing could be more sublime than that."

The Layman said, "So the teacher is someone who gives false compliments, is he?"

Pai-ling said, "Who doesn't? Who doesn't?"

The Layman bowed[1] and left.

---

1. A perfunctory parting gesture.

21. What Did You Say?

One day Pai-ling was doing meditation in his room when the Layman came into the temple.

As the Layman passed by his room, Pai-ling suddenly grabbed him and said, "People of the present day talk about it, and people of former times talked about it. What does the Layman have to say about it?"

The Layman slapped him.

Pai-ling said, "At least, you did say *something*."

The Layman said, "Where is the transgression in what I said?"

Pai-ling said, "It's in your hand, of course."

The Layman drew closer to him and said, "Take a close look at my hand."[1]

Pai-ling bowed.[2]

---

1. The slapping action has nothing to do with the Layman's hand.

2. A perfunctory parting gesture.

22. The Eyes

One day the Layman questioned Pai-ling, asking, "Can people avoid talking about what they see with their eyes?"

Pai-ling said, "How can it be avoided?"

The Layman said, "By knowing instantly! By knowing instantly!"

Pai-ling said, "The carefree man is never beaten by the stick."

The Layman twirled around, saying, "Beat me! Beat me!"

Pai-ling reached down and grabbed a stick, but the Layman snatched it from him and said, "So! Can you avoid seeing me?"

Pai-ling did not reply.

23. Haggling Over a Basket

One day, when the Layman went to visit Master Ta-t'ung P'u-chi (Daido Fuzai),[1] he held up a bamboo basket[2] and said, "Master Ta-t'ung! Master Ta-t'ung!"

When P'u-chi did not respond, the Layman said, "The Master's place is where the lineage of Shih-t'ou resides. Has the ice thawed and have the chunks floated away?"

P'u-chi said, "I don't want to quibble with old man P'ang about the obvious."

The Layman put down the basket and said, "Isn't it better to receive a scrap of knowledge than a bit of cash?"

P'u-chi said, "Even though he knows I haven't a bit of cash, he still wants to haggle over it."

The Layman did a little dance and started to leave when P'u-chi picked up the bamboo basket and said, "Layman!"

When the Layman turned around, P'u-chi did a little dance and left.

The Layman clapped his hands and said, "We're agreed!"[3]

1. Ta-t'ung P'u-chi, a dharma heir of Shih-t'ou, was a native of Hunan Province. Other than that, no information has been passed down about him.

2. The Layman and his family made bamboo baskets that they sold in the market to make money. In this anecdote he is pretending to be selling his wares "door to door."

3. This is a quotation from the chorus of a tune popular at the time, literally meaning "Let's go home together," which also has the idiomatic meaning of agreeing to terms. Here the line also refers to the fact that the Layman and P'u-chi are dharma brothers in the lineage of Shih-t'ou.

24. Speaking Words

One day, P'u-chi asked the Layman, "In former days and in present times, there have been very few people who have been able to refrain from talking about it. Right now, can the old man refrain from it?"[1]

The Layman responded with a deep sigh.

P'u-chi repeated the question and the Layman said, "I just told you."

P'u-chi repeated the question again and the Layman said, "I just told you."

P'u-chi said, "Not only right now, but in former times, people have said as much."

The Layman did a little dance and left.

P'u-chi said, "Such craziness is of our own creation, but is there anyone who can get the point of it?"[2]

1. Compare this with anecdotes 20 and 21, on pages 51 and 52, for different treatments of a similar theme.
2. This passage is difficult to translate. The sense of it is that the Zen experience is difficult to express and is something the inexperienced cannot appreciate. Slightly different versions of this last line appear in other texts.

25. A Word from the Womb

One day, when P'u-chi had come to visit him, the Layman asked him, "I would like to call the Master's attention to the time he was in his mother's womb.[1] Without relying on reasoning, can anything be said about it?"

P'u-chi said, "At birth we are removed from it."

The Layman said, "Please say something that does not rely on reasoning."

P'u-chi said, "I am not disposed to quibble over words with argumentative people."

The Layman said, "But if the Master's experience is clearly expressed, how could anyone argue with it?"

P'u-chi said, "Your 'not relying on reasoning' itself relies on reasoning."

The Layman said, "Now we are not only one birth but two births removed from it."

P'u-chi said, "A monk with his head buried in his bowl of gruel is getting the only point[2] he's supposed to get." The Layman snapped his fingers three times.

---

1. This is reminiscent of the famous question of the Sixth Patriarch, Hui-neng (Eno): "What is your original face before your parents were born?"

2. See the previous anecdote, where the same phrase—"get the point"—is used.

26. Open or Closed?

One day, when the Layman came to visit him, P'u-chi saw him coming and closed the door to his room, saying, "I don't care to see old man know-it-all today."

The Layman said, "Sitting alone and talking to yourself, you won't offend anyone, eh?"

P'u-chi started to open the door to come outside when the Layman grabbed it from him and slid it open, saying, "So, who's the know-it-all? The Master or me?"

P'u-chi said, "Setting aside the question of who's the know-it-all, as the door slides back and forth, how do you know whether it is open or closed?"

The Layman said, "This is the kind of question that chokes the life out of people."

P'u-chi laughed and the Layman said, "You've been playing me for a fool all along!"

27. Not Violating the True Self

When the Layman arrived at Zen Master Ch'ang-tzu's[1] place, the monks were assembling for a discourse as he entered the temple grounds.[2]

The Layman stood outside as the monks approached the lecture hall and said, "Each of you would do well to speak from your own experience."

As Ch'ang-tzu addressed the assembly, the Layman stood to the right side of the dais.[3]

When the discourse was finished, a monk asked, "Could the Master please speak without violating his true self?"[4]

Ch'ang-tzu said, "Are you acquainted with Mr. P'ang?"

The monk said, "I am not acquainted with him."

Thereupon, the Layman grabbed the monk by the lapels and said, "Is it that hard [to be acquainted with me]? Is it that hard?"

The monk could not reply, and the Layman let go of him.

Later, Ch'ang-tzu asked the Layman, "Would it be worthwhile taking the stick to that monk?"[5]

The Layman said, "What have you been waiting for?"

Ch'ang-tzu said, "The Layman only knows how to work with an awl; he doesn't know how to work with a chisel."[6]

The Layman said, "Then you wouldn't say something meaningful to a person if someone else overhearing it couldn't understand it?"

Ch'ang-tzu said, "Why wouldn't someone else understand it?"

The Layman said, "The Master only knows how to work with a chisel; he doesn't know how to work with an awl."

---

1. Chang-tzu was a dharma heir of Shih-t'ou. His temple was in T'an-chou (present-day Ch'ang-sha), the largest city in Hunan Province. Although anecdotes about him appear in other sources, including the text known as the "Transmission of the Lamp," (Chin.: *Chingte Ch'uanteng Lu*; Jpn.: *Keitoku Dento Roku*), nothing about his personal details have been passed down.

2. In those days, the Master's discourse was followed by a question-and-answer period.

3. The Layman assumes the position of Chang-tzu's attendant. An attendant stands to the right side of the dais as the Master speaks.

4. The term translated as "true self"—literally "the ruler that dwells within"—is one that occurs with some frequency in

Zen texts, most notably in the twelfth case of the *Wu-men-kuan* (*Mumonkan*).

5. Ch'ang-tzu is asking the Layman if he thinks the monk has enough potential for Ch'ang-tzu to make a special effort to help him along in his practice.

6. Here the metaphor is that an awl is used to punch a hole in something with one blow, whereas a chisel is used to chip away at something slowly.

28. Why Don't You Say Something?

While having tea with the priest Sung-shan,[1] the Layman held up the serving tray with the teacups on it and said, "Each person has a full share, so why don't they say anything about it?"

Sung-shan said, "It is just that each person has a full share that they say nothing about it."

The Layman said, "Why doesn't my elder brother[2] say something about it?"

Sung-shan said, "What is there to say about it?"

The Layman said, "It's obvious! It's obvious!"

Sung-shan then took a drink of tea.

The Layman said, "My elder brother drinks his tea without saluting[3] his guest."[4]

Sung-shan said, "Who is that?"

The Layman said, "Mr. P'ang!"

Sung-shan said, "What more of a salute would you like?"

Afterward, Tan-hsia[5] heard about this and said, "Sung-shan is someone who can confuse the old man before he can hoist one [cup of tea]."

Upon hearing this, the Layman called someone to take his reply to Tan-hsia and said, "What's the point of meeting if we never clink our cups?"[6]

I. Sung-shan was a disciple of Ma-tsu. Other than appearing in this text, Sung-shan is not mentioned in Zen literature.

2. This term, though having an air of informality, carries the feeling of respect while also acknowledging the priest (rather than master) status of Sung-shan.

3. "Saluting" refers to some kind of acknowledgment, such as a slight bow or offered toast.

4. The terms "host" and "guest" were developed in this period of the Zen heritage as metaphors for subject and object (absolute and relative). Later, an entire form of Zen dialogue about "host and guest" was developed by Master Lin-chi (Rinzai).

5. See the chapter "Dialogues with Tan-hsia," pages 35–47.

6. The "addenda" to this anecdote (the additions made by Tan-hsia and then the Layman to the initial encounter) provide a glimpse into the situation in the mountains where these men lived. They clearly lived in proximity to each other and were frequent visitors to each other's abodes.

29. The Ox Doesn't Know

One day, when the Layman and Sung-shan were out for a walk, they saw an ox plowing the fields. The Layman pointed to the ox and said, "He's having the time of his life, but he doesn't know anything about it."

Sung-shan said, "That is, unless Mr. P'ang wants to bring the issue to his attention."

The Layman said, "My master always said he never knew what he was doing."

Sung-shan said, "Since I never saw Shih-t'ou, it would be better if I didn't say anything about it."

The Layman said, "What would you have to say after you'd seen him?"

Sung-shan clapped his hands three times.[1]

---

1. This is done in a somewhat sarcastic manner.

30. Sung-shan's Staff

One day, when the Layman arrived at Sung-shan's place, he saw that Sung-shan was hewing a staff, so he said, "What's that in your hand?"

Sung-shan said, "The time has come when this old monk cannot even take one step without support from this."[1]

The Layman said, "Even though it has come to this, don't you still have some vitality left?"

Sung-shan then struck the Layman with the staff.

The Layman said, "Put down that staff for a moment and let me ask you something."

Sung-shan put down the staff and the Layman said, "Doesn't this old Chinaman have anything to say about what I just asked him?"

Sung-shan let out a shout.

The Layman said, "From out of the clear blue, suffering arises."

1. In the old days in China, there were regulations concerning at what ages a man could carry a staff in certain places—his neighborhood, within the city walls, at court, and so on. This was because a staff was considered a potential weapon.

31. Yellow Leaves and Green Leaves

One day, when the Layman and Sung-shan were out for a walk, they saw some monks picking greens, and Sung-shan said, "The yellow leaves are discarded while the green leaves are taken."

The Layman said, "Without noticing yellow or green, what do you make of it?"

Sung-shan said, "It's fine with me."

The Layman said, "Being either guest or host[1] can be difficult."

Sung-shan said, "What is brought into this world is compelled by something beyond."[2]

The Layman said, "This[3] is so for all of us, is it not?"

Sung-shan said, "So it is. So it is."

The Layman said, "Consequently, without noticing yellow or green, it is difficult to say anything."

Sung-shan laughed and said, "So, are you finished talking about this?"

The Layman bowed to the assembled monks [picking greens].

Sung-shan said, "The assembly invites your participation."

The Layman then left.

---

1. See anecdote 28, note 4, page 68.

2. The term "something beyond" refers to a deeper source to the animated world. This is an unusual reference in Zen texts, and the characters involved are not of common usage.

3. See anecdote 18, note 1, page 47, for "this."

32. Sung-shan's Ruler

One day, when Sung-shan was chatting with the Layman, he suddenly picked up a ruler that was on the table and said, "Do you see this?"

The Layman said, "I see it!"

Sung-shan said, "What do you see?"

The Layman said, "Sung-shan."

Sung-shan said, "Can you say it without speaking?"

The Layman said, "You're the one who's quibbling about not speaking."

Sung-shan put down the ruler, and the Layman said, "To have a head with no tail is regrettable."

Sung-shan said, "It is not so. Today the old man won't get there by speaking."

The Layman said, "Get to where?"

Sung-shan said, "To where there is a head but no tail."

The Layman said, "Being something [form] is the

weakness of strength; being nothing [emptiness] is the strength of weakness."

Sung-shan put his arm around the Layman and said, "You're always in an unspeakable place, aren't you, old man?"

33. Don't Tell Someone What to Do

The Layman asked the priest Pen-hsi,[1] "What do you make of Tan-hsia and the attendant who was hit?"[2]

Pen-hsi said, "An old man[3] can tell whether someone measures up or not."[4]

The Layman said, "Since I practiced together with the teacher, may I put forward a question?"

Pen-hsi said, "As you wish, please bring up an issue and I will evaluate it with you."

The Layman said, "Even for an old man, it isn't right to tell someone what they should or shouldn't do."

Pen-hsi said, "You should have respect for your elders."

The Layman said, "Oh, forgive me! Forgive me!"

---

1. Although this anecdote is repeated in several other texts, it is Pen-hsi's only appearance in the literature. Nothing has been passed down about him except that he and the Layman

were dharma brothers while studying with Ma-tsu (as inferred from the text).

2. This refers to an incident recorded in the "Transmission of
the Lamp." Tan-hsia had gone to see the National Teacher
(the spiritual advisor to the emperor) Nan-yang Hui-chung
(Nanyo Echu), a dharma heir of the Sixth Patriarch. (This
probably occurred around 774–775, as Nan-yang died in
775.) When Tan-hsia arrived, he asked Nan-yang's attendant if the teacher was in. The attendant said that he was,
but was not receiving any visitors. When Tan-hsia expressed
disappointment, the attendant said, "Why don't you see
him with your buddha eye?" Tan-hsia replied, "Dragons are
born of dragons and phoenixes are born of phoenixes," and
left. When the attendant told Nan-yang about this, Nan-
yang hit him. When Tan-hsia heard this, he said, "What a
guy the National Teacher is!" and returned to see him.

Another interesting aspect of this passage is that the
Layman is using an anecdotal story as a "test question"—a
practice that would become the standard Zen teaching
methodology in the Sung dynasty.

3. Referring to both Nan-yang and himself.

4. Literally, "whether someone is tall or short."

34. Is This So, or Not?

One day, Pen-hsi saw the Layman coming and stared at him for a long time. The Layman then drew a circle on the ground with his staff. Pen-hsi came forward and stood in the circle.

The Layman said, "Is this[1] so, or not?"

Pen-hsi then drew a circle on the ground in front of the Layman, and the Layman stood inside it.

Pen-hsi said, "Is this so, or not?"

The Layman threw down his staff and simply stood there.

Pen-hsi said, "You came with a staff. Are you leaving without it?"

The Layman said, "I am content here in the circle. Stare all you want; there's nothing to see."

Pen-hsi clapped his hands and said, "How extraordinary! He's not here anymore."

The Layman picked up his staff and left.
Pen-hsi said, "Don't forget the way back!"

---

1. See anecdote 18, note 1, for "'this.'"

35. The Plum's Core

The Layman went to visit Zen Master Ta-mei.[1] As they were about to exchange greetings, the Layman said, "It has taken a while for the big plum tree[2] to mature. I wonder if any of the plums are ripe yet?"

Ta-mei said, "Go ahead and try one."

The Layman said, "How completely unique!"

Ta-mei opened his arms wide and said, "You've gotten to the core!"

---

1. Ta-mei Fa-ch'ang (Daibai Hojo) was a dharma heir of Ma-tsu. He lived at Yu-chuan Temple (Jpn.: Hosen-ji) in the Ching-chou district of Hunan. He is well known as the monk who asked Ma-tsu the question "What is buddha?" eliciting the reply "Mind is buddha." After Ta-mei had established his temple in Hunan, Ma-tsu sent a monk to visit him with the message that "Ma-tsu now says, 'No mind, no buddha.'" Ta-mei replied, "That old rascal Ma-tsu is just

trying to confuse people!" When the monk returned and told Ma-tsu of this, Ma-tsu said, "Ah, the plums have ripened!" (A play on Ta-mei's name, which means "big plum tree").

2. The Layman's question is a play on Ta-mei's name.

36. Dining Etiquette

When the Layman went to Zen Master Ta-yu's[1] place on Mount Fu-yang, they sat down for lunch together. Just as the Layman was about to serve himself from one of the pots, Ta-yu grabbed his arm and said, "The *Vimalakirti Sutra* speaks about the mind being nourished by whatever is given.[2] Your action [of serving yourself] betrays this. Does the Layman go along with it or not?"

The Layman said, "Didn't Subhuti[3] get his fill at that moment?"

Ta-yu said, "But we're not talking about him."

The Layman said, "When I put food in my mouth, everyone is given sustenance."

Ta-yu then stopped eating.

The Layman said, "Please! Finish what you were saying."

---

1. Ta-yu of Mount Fu-yang (745–825) was a dharma heir of

Ma-tsu. He became a monk at the age of twelve and entered An-kuo Temple (Ankoku-ji) in the T'ang capital of Ch'ang-an when he was twenty-three. Afterward he studied with Ma-tsu. In 818 he went to live at Mount Fu-yang (in present-day Jiangsu Province), where he is thought to have died around 825, at the age of eighty. It is not known where he was living when the meeting documented here took place.

2. As Ta-yu was a dharma brother of the Layman's (as fellow disciples of Ma-tsu), their meal together was, of course, informal. However, Ta-yu draws on his extensive experience of monastic etiquette to try to catch the Layman napping. He brings up a point of Buddhist monastic etiquette that harks back to ancient scripture. The reference is to a passage where Vimalakirti—the archetypical "enlightened layman"—teaches the dharma to Subhuti (see anecdote 19, note 4) while filling his begging bowl. In formal monastic meals, the monks are always served; they do not serve themselves. This reflects the principle that monks only eat what others provide for them and are supposed to eat whatever comes into their begging bowls.

3. The Layman counters Ta-yu, showing that he knows the scriptural point that Ta-yu is referring to. Subhuti was one of the Buddha's sixteen disciples.

37. Fundamental Truth

Another time, the Layman asked Ta-yu, "In order to help others attain it, Master Ma-tsu dwelt in the fundamental reality. Did he pass this on to you or not?"[1]

Ta-yu said, "Since I have never spoken with him, how could I know anything about his fundamental reality?"

The Layman said, "Then you have nothing to report about this experience?"

Ta-yu said, "I don't have one word to give to the Layman on the subject."

The Layman said, "If the teacher would be forsaking the heritage by giving me one word about it, perhaps he can describe it to me in two or three words."

Ta-yu said, "That it can't be described is exactly what the fundamental reality is all about."

The Layman clapped his hands and left.

1. In the "Transmission of the Lamp" it is said that Ta-yu received his sanction as a Zen master from Ma-tsu secretly. The Layman's inquiry is about this secret transmission.

38. Old and Young

When the Layman was visiting with him, the priest Tse-ch'uan[1] asked, "Is it true that you grasped Shih-t'ou's teaching the first time you met him, or not?"[2]

The Layman said, "What sort of gossip has the teacher heard about this?"

Tse-ch'uan said, "What is known instantly,[3] but takes a long time to fully realize, is a gradual process."

The Layman said, "Old Tse-ch'uan is much further along in years than Mr. P'ang."

Tse-ch'uan said, "But we are both here wrangling over this issue."

The Layman said, "Surely the youthful Mr. P'ang will prevail over the teacher."

Tse-ch'uan said, "Even though you may prevail, you'd still be wearing that silly head scarf."

The Layman removed his head scarf and said, "Now I look just like the teacher."

Tse-ch'uan laughed heartily.

---

1. Tse-ch'uan was a disciple of Ma-tsu and came from Sze-chuan (present-day Sichuan), as implied by his name. Other than that, nothing has been passed down about him.

2. See anecdote 1, note 2.

3. See anecdote 22 for "knowing instantly."

39. The Intangible Dharma Body

One day, while the Layman and Tse-ch'uan were having tea, the Layman said, "The dharma body[1] is intangible. Can the teacher see mine or not?"

Tse-ch'uan said, "It is not for this old monk to say anything about that of which you speak."

The Layman said, "That a question has an answer is the normal way of things."

Tse-ch'uan just sipped his tea as if he didn't hear anything, so the Layman said, "Don't be so obtuse! I'm just asking a simple question."

Tse-ch'uan ignored him.

The Layman then raised his voice and said, "The old Chinaman is so impolite! I thought I was talking to someone who could see with both eyes!"

Tse-ch'uan threw out the rest of his tea and went to his room.

1. The dharma body, or *dharmakaya*, is one of the three aspects, or "bodies," of the all-inclusive *buddhakaya* in traditional (scriptural) Buddhist philosophy. The *dharmakaya* is the essential aspect; the *nirmanakaya* is the material aspect; and the *sambhogakaya* is the psycho-emotional aspect that arises from the interplay of the other two.

40. Host and Guest

One day, the Layman arrived while Tse-ch'uan was meditating in his room. The Layman said, "If you simply stay
in your room, absorbed in meditation, how can you know
when a monk has come to see you?"

Tse-ch'uan uncrossed one leg.[1]

The Layman turned to leave, but after taking a few
steps he turned back around. Tse-ch'uan then recrossed
his leg.

The Layman said, "Do you call this "freely being yourself"?

Tse-ch'uan said, "I am being the host."[2]

The Layman said, "The elder teacher only knows how
to be the host. He doesn't know how to be the guest."

Tse-ch'uan then called to his attendant to bring some
tea, and the Layman did a little dance and left.

1. He started to get up from his cross-legged meditation position.
2. See anecdote 28, note 4.

41. Hot and Cold

When he arrived at Zen Master Lo-p'u's[1] place, after he had bowed in greeting, the Layman said, "Sweating in the heat by May and shivering in the cold by October."

Lo-p'u said, "What's wrong with that?"

The Layman said, "Mr. P'ang is getting along in years."

Lo-p'u said, "Why not just acknowledge that it's cold when it's cold and it's hot when it's hot?"

The Layman said, "What do you say about old age, then?"

Lo-p'u said, "I'll spare you from twenty blows [of the stick]."[2]

The Layman said, "My speech may be getting a little slurred, but your eyesight is failing."[3]

---

1. Lo-p'u Yuan-an (Rakuho Genan, 734–798) was a dharma heir of Chia-shan Shan-hui (Kassan Zenne). His temple was in the Li-chou district of Hunan.

2. This is a figurative expression meaning "If I had my stick in my hand, I'd beat you." The phrase "spare you from twenty blows" means sparing you for the moment—the blows will be delivered later.

3. The Layman is implying that with Lo-p'u's failing eyesight (they are both elderly), he probably couldn't hit the Layman anyway.

42. Tan-hsia's Activities

When the Layman went to the priest Shih-lin's[1] place, Shih-lin saw him coming and held up his whisk,[2] saying, "Without using any of Tan-hsia's[3] actions can you say something [about him] that is to the point?"

The Layman grabbed the whisk from Shih-lin's hand, then quickly offered it back to him again.

Shih-lin said, "This is an action of Tan-hsia."

The Layman said, "Have you lost the use of your eyes so you can't tell who I am?"

Shih-lin said, "Tan-hsia's speech is slurred and the Layman is hard of hearing."

The Layman said, "Clearly!"

Shih-lin did not reply, so the Layman said, "Weren't you going on about something just now?"

Shih-lin did not reply.[4]

1. Shih-lin was a disciple of Ma-tsu. Other than this, nothing has been passed down about him.

2. See anecdote 13, note 1, page 39.

3. See the chapter "Dialogues with Tan-hsia," pages 35–47.

4. This anecdote, like anecdote 28, shows that the Zen men in the hills of Hunan were quite well known to one another.

43. Say It Succinctly

One day, Shih-lin questioned the Layman, saying, "There's something I must ask. Does the Layman ever say anything succinctly?"

The Layman said, "Could you please tell me exactly what it is you're quibbling about?"

Shih-lin said, "I just asked you to say something succinct!"

The Layman said, "Doesn't your question presume someone is going to understand it [when I say it]?"

Shih-lin covered his ears.

The Layman said, "How concise! How concise!"

44. It's Indescribable

One day, Shih-lin and the Layman were having tea. Just as the Layman was about to take a sip, Shih-lin held his arm back and said, "What does it taste like?"

The Layman said, "It's indescribable."

Shih-lin said, "Surely you can compare it to something."

The Layman pulled his sleeve from Shih-lin's grasp, got up from his seat, and said, "It's wholly unique."

Shih-lin said, "So old P'ang knows what it's like, then."

The Layman turned to leave, and Shih-lin said, "It's wholly unique."

The Layman did not reply, so Shih-lin said, "Finally, you're speechless!"

45. Respected Mountain

When the Layman visited Zen Master Yang-shan[1] he asked him, "People are always paying respect to the mountain.[2] Now that I'm here, I wonder if the mountain reciprocates."

Yang-shan held up his whisk.[3]

The Layman said, "Clearly!"[4]

Yang-shan said, "The respect is reciprocated."

The Layman slapped the wooden post next to him and said, "Though this wood post is not human, it can still bear witness."

Yang-shan then put down his whisk and said, "Wherever we may go, our only duty is to be respectful."

---

1. Except for this anecdote, Yang-shan does not appear in Zen literature. This Yang-shan is not to be confused with

the well-known dharma heir of Kuei-shan (Isan), Yang-shan Hui-chi (Kyozan Ejaku), who lived during the ninth century.

2. The Layman is playing on Yang-shan's name, which means "respected mountain."

3. See anecdote 13, note 1, page 39.

4. See anecdote 42 for "Clearly!"

46. Wild Fox Zen

When the Layman went to visit the Taoist Ku-yin,[1] Ku-yin asked him, "Who are you?"

The Layman raised his staff.

Ku-yin said, "But this is only the act of raising something up."

The Layman lowered his staff, but Ku-yin said nothing.

The Layman said, "You only know about the act of something being raised up. You don't know about the meaning of its being raised up."

Ku-yin said, "What is the meaning of its being raised up?"

The Layman raised his staff.

Ku-yin said, "This is frivolous."

The Layman said, "How sad that I can't perform any better for my lord."[2]

Ku-yin said, "I am a person who has but one activity. I don't need to lift things up or put them down. I have no use for repartee or idle chatter. If the Layman is to confront me, how will he do it?"

The Layman said, "Where shall the confrontation occur?"

Ku-yin then grabbed the Layman by the lapels.

The Layman said, "Is this all there is to it or not?" Then, after a moment, he spat in Ku-yin's face.

Ku-yin did not reply.

The Layman then composed a verse:

In glittering noonday waters,
There are no fish to catch.
When my lord sees there are no fish,
He may know they are laughing at his plight.
How sad that Ku-yin hooked onto his elder Zen brother
And had to get spat upon in order to realize his foolishness.

---

1. Little is known about Ku-yin, but there is a mountain in Hsiang-yang, the Layman's hometown, known as Mount Ku-yin (Hidden Valley), which may have been named after him. He is said to have been a Taoist, though in T'ang times the term *Taoist* also meant a hermit.

2. The Layman is being sarcastic.

47. Reading the Sutras

When the Layman was lying down on the meditation platform reading sutras, a monk saw him and said, "Doesn't the Layman know that he should maintain proper posture when reading the sutras?"[1]

The Layman propped up one leg.

The monk said nothing.

---

1. Here, the Layman is probably visiting the temple of one of his friends.

DIALOGUE WITH A MONK
DOING RITUAL BEGGING

48. Accepting Charity

One day, the Layman was selling his bamboo wares in the market in the town of Hung-chou when he saw a monk on his ritual begging rounds. The Layman held out a coin for him, saying, "Can you tell me about the teaching of not being ungrateful for whatever is handed out to you?[1] If you can say something, I will give you this coin."

The monk did not reply, so the Layman said, "You ask me the question and I'll answer it for you."

The monk said, "What is the teaching of not being ungrateful for whatever is handed out to you?"

The Layman said, "Hardly anyone can accept it." Then he added, "Do you understand?"

The monk said, "I don't understand."

The Layman said, "Who is it that hasn't understood?"

1. This anecdote reflects the same principle of Buddhism that was touched upon in the dialogue with Ta-yu (see anecdote 36, note 2).

49. Where the Path Leads

One day the Layman saw a young boy herding oxen and asked him, "Where does this path we're following lead to?"

The boy said, "I don't know where it goes."

The Layman said, "Aren't you herding the oxen?"

The boy said, "They live in these fields."[1]

The Layman said, "What time of day is it anyway?"

The boy said, "It's time to take the oxen to pasture."

The Layman laughed heartily.

---

1. The sense of this statement is that the oxen know where they are going.

50. The Message of the *Diamond Sutra*

The Layman dropped in at a temple where a priest was giving a public lecture on the *Diamond Sutra*. When the priest came to the part that says "There is no I and there is no other," the Layman asked the priest, "About the part that says, 'There is no I and there is no other,' who then is lecturing now and who is listening to it?"

The priest did not reply, so the Layman said, "I am only a layperson, but I have a rough idea about the teaching involved."

The priest said, "So what are the Layman's thoughts about it?"

The Layman then composed a verse:

"There is no I and there is no other."
How can there be intimacy or estrangement?
I recommend giving up trying to get there by meditation,
But rather, directly seizing the reality at hand.

The message of the *Diamond Sutra* is:
Nothing is excluded from our experienced world.
From beginning to end,
It inevitably exposes our false identities.

Upon hearing this verse, the priest was delighted and expressed his gratitude.

Wherever the Layman went, whether it was a place he frequented or was just passing through, his actions were always appropriate to the situation. He was always unpredictable and spontaneous.

51. Three Views of Hard and Easy

One day, while the Layman was meditating in his sitting hut, he suddenly cried out, "It's hard, hard, hard! And I've put ten coats of linseed oil on this platform, too!"

His wife said, "It's easy, easy, easy! Just turn your eyes to the floor, lower your feet to it, and be on your way!"

Ling-chao said, "It's neither hard nor easy! The mind of the Patriarchs is in every blade of grass!"[1]

---

1. The Layman's daughter, Ling-chao, is referring to a line from the Third Patriarch's work the "Treatise on Believing in Mind" (Chin.: *Hsin-hsin ming;* Jpn.: *Shinjin-mei*) that says, "Though the Great Way is expansive, treading upon it is neither hard nor easy." Also, see anecdote 53. Very little has been passed down about the life details of the Third Patriarch, Chien-chih Seng-ts'an (Kanchi Sosan, ?–606), who stood halfway between Bodhidharma and Hui-neng.

52. Three-Stanza Poem

At the beginning of the Yuan-he period,[1] the Layman moved into a cottage he built on the north bank of the Hsiang River.[2] He worked with his daughter, Ling-chao, making bamboo baskets. They were together morning and night. The Layman had a verse that went:

> The mind is like a reflection in a mirror:
> Though it is insubstantial, it is not nonexistent.
> What is, we have no control over;
> And what isn't, is ephemeral.
> Aren't the esteemed sages
> Just regular people who've resolved this matter?
>
> There are changes upon changes.
> Once the five components[3] are clearly seen,
> The diverse things in the world are joined into one.

How can there be two formless dharma bodies?[4]
Once compulsive desires[5] are eliminated and insight comes,
There are no thoughts about where the promised land[6]
    may lie.

The will to survive must be killed off.
Once it is killed off, there will be peace of mind.
When the mind integrates this,
An iron ship has been made to float.[7]

---

1. The Yuan-he period ran from 806–821. Since the Layman
   passed away in 808, the circumstance described here must
   have occurred near the end of his life.

2. The timing of this brief account corresponds with the timing in the Prologue where the Layman is described as
   "camping out" on a cliff ledge.

3. This second stanza is filled with references to Buddhist philosophy. The five components are the five *skandhas* that are
   involved in the existence of a human being according to old
   Buddhist texts. They are form (the physical body), emo-
   tion, thought, intention, and consciousness.

4. The term "dharma body" occurs previously, in anecdote
   39. Here the Layman uses the term in its full philosophical
   expression, "formless dharma body." This refers to the uni-
   versal underlying substrate of being.

5. "Compulsive desires" are the source of suffering according
   to the Buddha's teaching. Being free from their influence is
   the first step toward nirvana.

6. The "promised land" is an interpretation of the term "buddha realm," or the experience of enlightened mind.

7. In the Layman's time it was thought that it would be impossible for an iron ship to float.

53. Each Blade of Grass Is Clear-Cut

One day, while they were meditating, the Layman turned to Ling-chao and said, "There is a man of old who said, 'Each blade of grass is clear-cut, the mind of the Patriarchs is clear-cut.'[1] What is your understanding of this?"

Ling-chao said, "Our old friend[2] has said it well."

The Layman said, "But what about you?"

Ling-chao said, "Each blade of grass is clear-cut, the mind of the Patriarchs is clear-cut."

The Layman laughed.

---

1. This is a quotation from the "Treatise on Believing in Mind," mentioned in anecdote 51, note 1.

2. In the phrase quoted by the Layman, the term translated as "clear-cut" is a repeated character (*ming-ming:* the character for "bright" repeated). Ling-chao, in her reply here, plays upon this by doubling the characters translated as "old friend" in a unique and creative way.

54. Helping Someone Up

Once, when the Layman was on his way to sell his bamboo baskets, he stumbled and fell while crossing over a bridge. When Ling-chao saw this, she came to her father's side and fell on the ground.

The Layman said, "What are you doing?"

Ling-chao said, "I saw you had fallen, so I came to lend you a hand."

The Layman said, "But who can see what there is to take hold of?"

55. The Layman's Death

When the Layman was in his final days, he called Ling-chao to him and said, "As the day turns from morning to night, can it be said when it has reached halfway [when it is noon]?"

Ling-chao went into the garden and said, "It is midday, yet there is some obscurity."

When he went outside, the Layman saw Ling-chao sitting in meditation on his meditation bench, but she had died. The layman laughed and said, "My girl has fitted the arrowhead to the shaft."

After a week had gone by, Governor Yu came to inquire about the Layman's illness, and the Layman recited a verse:

Our hollow desires
Comprise what is something [form].
The awareness that has no substance

Comprises what is nothing [emptiness].
A good day in the world
Is but a side effect.

After reciting the verse, the Layman laid his head in the governor's lap and passed away. Later, according to the Layman's wishes, his body was cremated and the ashes were scattered in the river.

Monks and laypeople alike mourned the Layman's passing, and he was posthumously given the sangha name Wei-ma (Yuima).[2] The Layman's legacy included over three hundred poems that are in circulation in the world.[3]

---

1. Compare this account of the Layman's death with that presented in the Prologue. In addition, as Professor Iriya points out, there are widely varying versions of the Layman's and Ling-chao's deaths given in other old Zen texts. However, inasmuch as Governor Yu is considered to have compiled the original edition of the text, the account given here—which does *not* include the segment about his wife and son—should be given more weight than that of the Prologue.

2. *Wei-ma* is the Chinese version of the Sanskrit *Vimalakirti*. Vimalakirti is the prototypical "enlightened layman" of Buddhism, and the *Vimalakirti Nirdesha Sutra* is one of the earliest writings considered to be part of the Buddhist canon.

3. See the Introduction for a discussion about the "missing" poems of the Layman.

56. Tan-hsia's Rosary

One day, while Tan-hsia was holding a rosary in his hand, the Layman came up to him and grabbed hold of it, saying, "Now neither of us is empty-handed."

Tan-hsia said, "The covetous old man doesn't know right from wrong."

The Layman said, "But the Master has yet to give testimony for my arrest. What will he say when it comes down to it?"

Tan-hsia said, "Oh, boo-hoo! Boo-hoo!"[2]

The Layman said, "What a crybaby the Master is!"

Tan-hsia said, "Where's my stick?"

The Layman said, "You wouldn't beat an old man, would you?"

Tan-hsia said, "A Chinaman who's numb to pain deserves to be beaten mercilessly."

The Layman said, "Have you no other means to make me give up possession?"

Tan-hsia then let go of the rosary and walked away.

The Layman said, "Stop, thief! How can someone steal what is freely given?"

Tan-hsia turned around and laughed heartily.

The Layman said, "So! The thief has been caught out!"

Tan-hsia then came up to the Layman and grabbed him by the lapels, saying, "Do you have anything else up your sleeve?"

The Layman slapped him.

---

1. The three dialogues in this chapter did not appear in the original text but were culled from other sources by the meticulous researches of Professor Iriya.

2. Tan-hsia is pretending to cry.

57. Pen-hsi and the Skull

The priest Pen-hsi[1] asked the Layman, "Do you have a word to say about Bodhidharma's[2] coming from the West?"[3]

The Layman said, "Does anyone remember it?"

Pen-hsi said, "How can you say the spirit of it hasn't been remembered?"

The Layman said, "How can I know about ancient times? I don't even know East from West."

Pen-hsi said, "But it's happening right now."

The Layman said, "I can't find a word for it."

Pen-hsi said, "Wise men of former times have talked about it and shed light on it for others."

The Layman said, "My teacher has very sharp eyes."

Pen-hsi said, "So it is, when you begin to talk about the ineffable!"

The Layman said, "Maybe there's something your eye doesn't see."

Pen-hsi said, "You can't quibble about my eyesight in the noonday sun!"

The Layman said, "It goes right through my skull."

Pen-hsi said, "So you've noticed it, then."

The Layman said, "What could this Chinaman possibly have that is unique?"[4]

Pen-hsi returned to his room.

---

1. See the chapter "Dialogues with Pen-hsi," pages 77–80, and anecdote 33, note 1.

2. Bodhidharma (Chin.: Ta-mo; Jpn.: Daruma) was the First Patriarch of Zen in China. He traveled from sixth-century India along the Silk Road, thus coming to China from the West.

3. This is a Zen "testing question" from the old days. In Zen lore it is said that Bodhidharma came from the West "directly pointing at the mind."

4. In this context, the word "unique" also refers to the original request that the Layman say a word about Bodhidharma's coming from the West.

58. Mrs. P'ang Goes Back

Mrs. P'ang happened to enter Lu-men Temple[1] during mealtime.

The gatekeeper called out for her to go back outside.[2]

Mrs. P'ang took the comb out of her hair and swept up her footprints behind her with her trailing long hair, saying, "I've gone back," and left.

---

1. In the Prologue it is said that the Layman went to live on a cliff ledge near Mount Lu-men, which was the site of this temple.
2. The monk gatekeeper had a special chant that alerted visitors to the fact that it was mealtime, indicating that they should come back later.

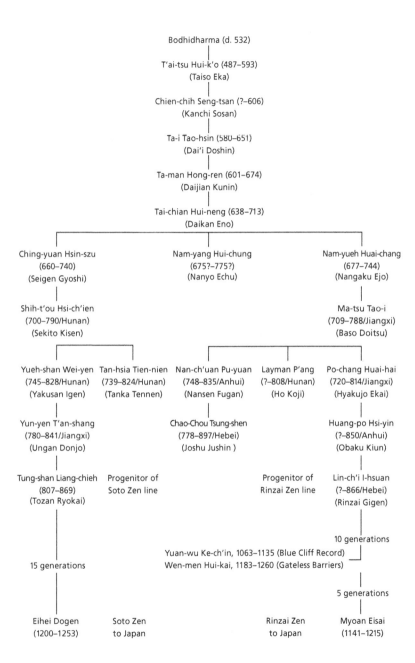

Bodhidharma (d. 532)

T'ai-tsu Hui-k'o (487–593)
(Taiso Eka)

Chien-chih Seng-tsan (?–606)
(Kanchi Sosan)

Ta-i Tao-hsin (580–651)
(Dai'i Doshin)

Ta-man Hong-ren (601–674)
(Daijian Kunin)

Tai-chian Hui-neng (638–713)
(Daikan Eno)

Ching-yuan Hsin-szu
(660–740)
(Seigen Gyoshi)

Nam-yang Hui-chung
(675?–775?)
(Nanyo Echu)

Nam-yueh Huai-chang
(677–744)
(Nangaku Ejo)

Shih-t'ou Hsi-ch'ien
(700–790/Hunan)
(Sekito Kisen)

Ma-tsu Tao-i
(709–788/Jiangxi)
(Baso Doitsu)

Yueh-shan Wei-yen
(745–828/Hunan)
(Yakusan Igen)

Tan-hsia Tien-nien
(739–824/Hunan)
(Tanka Tennen)

Nan-ch'uan Pu-yuan
(748–835/Anhui)
(Nansen Fugan)

Layman P'ang
(?–808/Hunan)
(Ho Koji)

Po-chang Huai-hai
(720–814/Jiangxi)
(Hyakujo Ekai)

Yun-yen T'an-shang
(780–841/Jiangxi)
(Ungan Donjo)

Chao-Chou Tsung-shen
(778–897/Hebei)
(Joshu Jushin)

Huang-po Hsi-yin
(?–850/Anhui)
(Obaku Kiun)

Tung-shan Liang-chieh
(807–869)
(Tozan Ryokai)

Progenitor of
Soto Zen line

Progenitor of
Rinzai Zen line

Lin-ch'i I-hsuan
(?–866/Hebei)
(Rinzai Gigen)

10 generations

Yuan-wu Ke-ch'in, 1063–1135 (Blue Cliff Record)
Wen-men Hui-kai, 1183–1260 (Gateless Barriers)

5 generations

15 generations

Eihei Dogen
(1200–1253)

Soto Zen
to Japan

Rinzai Zen
to Japan

Myoan Eisai
(1141–1215)

Brief Ancestor Chart

Bodhidharma arrived at a time of relative political insta-
bility in China, and the first few generations of his dharma
heirs were not very well known, nor could they be. During
the time of the Third Patriarch particularly, Buddhism
was severely persecuted. By the time of the Fourth Patriarch, however, the T'ang dynasty was well under way.

Although the early Patriarchs were based near the major
cities of Ch'ang-an (Xi'an) and Luo-yang (Loyang), the
Sixth Patriarch returned to his homeland in Canton
(Guangzhou). Although the Fifth Patriarch had other
dharma heirs, their lines—the Northern school—died
out. It is the Sixth Patriarch's line—the Southern school or
Sudden Illumination school—that continues to this day.

The T'ang dynasty began to break up in 874–875,
shortly after death of Lin-chi and Tung-shan. Nearly one
hundred years of turmoil followed until the Sung dynasty
began in 960. This time of chaos effectively divided the

Zen sect into two halves once again, with the Lin-chi (Rinzai) line establishing itself in the North and the Tung-shan (Soto) line in the South. It was the Lin-chi line that began using historical anecdotes (koan) as teaching devices during this time. This practice was codified in the "Blue Cliff Records" and "Gateless Barriers" collections of anecdotes about the T'ang masters.

After 1127, the Sung dynasty was pushed south of the Huai River, and the "barbarian" Ch'in (Northern Sung) dynasty was established to the north of the Huai. As a result, many of the monks based in northern China moved to the South.

Both Japanese monks—first Myoan Eisai, then Eihei Dogen—studied at temples in the province of Zhejiang, in the Southern Sung–controlled area of China.